Poverty or Prosperity?

Tax, Public Spending and Economic Recovery

Vito Tanzi
Irwin Stelzer
Peter Birch Sørenson
Dennis Snower
Deepak Lal
Alessio Brown
Arij Lans Bovenberg

Edited by Sheila Lawlor

imprint-academic.com

POLITEIA
2010

First published in 2010
by
Politeia and Imprint Academic
22 Charing Cross Road
London WC2H 0QP
Tel: 020 7240 5070 Fax: 020 7240 5095
E-mail: info@politeia.co.uk
Website: www.politeia.co.uk

ISBN 978 184540 196 2

Support for this study has been granted by
The Foundation for Social and Economic Thinking
The Institute for Policy Research

FTI Consulting*

Printed in Great Britain by:

Imprint Academic
PO Box 200
Exeter
Devon
EX5 5YK
United Kingdom

THE AUTHORS

Sheila Lawlor is Director of Politeia where she directs the economic and social policy programme. She writes on education, health and social security policy and has edited Politeia's series *Comparing Standards* series. Her books include *Churchill and the Politics of War, 1940-41* and she is currently writing a book on post-war social policy.

Vito Tanzi was Director of Fiscal Affairs at the IMF from 1981 until 2000. His publications include *Public Spending in the 20th Century: A Global Perspective* (Cambridge, 2000) with Ludger Schuknecht and, for Politeia, *Regulating for the New Economic Order: The Good, the Bad and the Damaging* (2008). He is currently writing a book on the role of the state in the economy.

Irwin Stelzer is Director of Economic Policy Studies at the Hudson Institute in Washington and a columnist both in the US and London where he writes for *The Sunday Times*. His academic career has been mainly in the US, where he has taught at Cornell University, the University of Connecticut and New York University. He has written widely on economic, regulatory and anti-trust law subjects.

Deepak Lal is the James S Coleman Professor of International Development Studies at the University of California, Los Angeles. His recent publications include *In Praise of Empires* (Palgrave Macmillan, 2004) *Reviving the Invisible Hand: The Case for Classical Liberalism in the 21st Century* (Princeton University Press, 2006).

Peter Birch Sørensen is Professor of Economics at the University of Copenhagen. He is Chairman of the Danish Economic Council, which advises the Danish Government and Parliament, having previously served as its Co-Chairman. He has been Director of Denmark's Economic Policy Research Unit (1998-2005) and a consultant on tax policy to the International Monetary Fund (IMF) as well as to the Canadian, Norwegian and Swedish governments. He writes on tax, social insurance and labour market reform. His co-author Professor Arij Lans Bovenberg is Scientific Director of Netspar at Tilburg University in the Netherlands having been the Director of the Centre for Economic Research at Tilburg University.

Dennis Snower is President of the Kiel Institute for the World Economy and Professor of Economics at the University of Kiel, Germany. Before that he was Chairman of the Department of Economics at Birkbeck College. His work examines the operation of labour markets and the welfare state. Recent books include *The Effects of Globalization on National Labor Markets: Diagnosis and Therapy*, (ed.) with Rainer Winkelmann and Klaus Zimmerman (Berlin, 2006). His co-author Alessio Brown is Head of the research area 'Reforming the Welfare State' at the Kiel Institute for the World Economy and executive director of the Global Economic Symposium.

FTI is an international consulting business that helps companies and their stakeholders protect and enhance enterprise value in an increasingly complex economic, legal and regulatory environment.

We are organised around five core practices: economic consulting, corporate finance, forensic and litigation consulting, strategic communications and technology.

FTI economic consulting provides law firms, corporations and government clients with clear analysis of complex economic issues for use in legal and regulatory proceedings, strategic decisions and public policy debates.

Chris Osborne, Senior Managing Director, FTI
Chris.osborne@fticonsulting.com

CONTENTS

Introduction - Looking Ahead: The Global   Sheila Lawlor   1
Economic Context

I   Taxing Trends: The Economic Role of the State   Vito Tanzi   5

II   Taxes in a Global Economy: Efficiency, Fairness   Irwin Stelzer   31
and Incentives

III   Tackling the Predatory State: From High Tax   Deepak Lal   47
Dirigisme to a New Liberalism

IV   Tax and Benefits for the Future: Social Accounts   Peter Birch Sørensen   66
in an Efficient, Fair Tax Transfer System   Arij Lans Bovenberg

V   Tax Reforms and Social Accounts: Incentives   Alessio J.G. Brown   104
for Efficient Re-distribution   Dennis J. Snower

Introduction
Looking Ahead: The Global Economic Context

Sheila Lawlor

Over the last ten years public spending, debt and tax in the UK have been rising as a proportion of GDP. Even before the financial crisis of 2007-8, the UK had been warned by the IMF about its levels of public spending. This deterioration in Britain's public finances in the decade before 2008 contributed to the severity of the economic crisis in the UK and has made recovery more difficult. The problems were exacerbated when, in response to the financial crash, government spending rose further. As a result the UK's public debt will be around 86 per cent of GDP by 2010 (*source, European Commission 2009 spring forecast, in L Schuknecht, *Boom, Bust and Fiscal Policy: Public finances in the future*, Politeia 2009).

But the problems do not end there. In common with other Western economies, the UK will, in the decades to come, face shrinking tax revenues and additional public spending demands. As in other Western economies, tax revenue will be under pressure from a global economy: taxpayers can move themselves or their capital to lower-cost economies - and so can jobs and investment. At the same time additional demands for public spending will arise with changing demography and an ageing population. As a result the UK could face the difficult combination of large fiscal imbalances and burgeoning demands on the public purse with the likelihood that the revenue available to government will fall.

This means that not only are the increases in tax and public spending over the 1990s and 2000s (including those of 2008/9) unsustainable, but different circumstances will determine future revenue and public spending.

But these problems can be surmounted, as the authors explain. The tax system reflects supply and demand, as well as responding to social, cultural and political pressures. Taxes that penalise incentive and hold back economic growth should be avoided, as should those which deter saving and investment, and those which are too complex. Taxes on 'bads', e.g. pollution, should be preferred to taxes on commodities and consumption. Within this framework, it is possible to respond to added pressures to expand public services or for more spending on benefits. In the case of healthcare, the government's role would be restricted to regulating and encouraging markets to provide and compete. Individuals would pay less tax but be expected to use the sums saved for their own healthcare. Benefits would be turned into individually owned welfare accounts, which could both ensure provision in times of need (such as unemployment) and also become a valuable asset for those who contribute to them.

The chapters which follow consider these questions under two broad headings: *Tax and public pending: reversible trends* and *The future of welfare?* They develop the following themes:

Tax and public spending: reversible trends
Vito Tanzi's analysis of tax trends over the 20th century shows that levels of tax and public spending have historically been inter-related, the result of both supply and demand and social, cultural and political trends. They rose from 10-12 per cent of GDP at the start of the 20th century to 40-50 per cent by the 1970s. Demand for tax revenue rose as the role of the state expanded, with the introduction of universal suffrage and the impact of two world wars. The supply of tax also increased: collection became easier; the proportion paying income tax rose with easily-taxable salary and wage packets, and from the 1960s newer taxes were used, with VAT providing almost 10 per cent of GDP revenue by 2001. By 1965 tax revenue as a share of GDP had grown to an average of 30 per cent in a range of Western countries including the UK, France and Germany. Over the next 20 years the proportion rose to 45 per cent of GDP by 1985, mainly due to VAT, the growth in social security contributions, and the increase in real incomes and in prices.

However, the high tax climate began to change as the economic consequences of high tax regimes and the complexity and instability of tax systems became evident. After reaching a peak in 1985, average tax levels fell and the focus shifted to more simplified tax systems, restructuring personal income tax and flatter tax rates.

Tax levels have, therefore, reflected changing fiscal and socio-political circumstances; and as Western countries face demographic change, there are fears that the levels will rise in response to additional demand. Such demand, can, however, be controlled, by transferring provision from government to the more efficient and sophisticated private markets and reallocating funding. The pressure to cut costs will be reinforced by the dwindling supply of tax - on account of foreign competition, globalisation and technology - and the changing structure of economies where capital income, more difficult to tax, will matter more than wages.

Irwin Stelzer suggests governments may have reached the limits of tax revenue. Today's global economy leads to greater mobility of both labour and capital. High earners can leave high tax regimes and investors move their capital. Those who remain will not wish to pay or vote for higher taxes. If governments are to maintain or raise their income, there are three options, all of which may be difficult: they will have to cut spending, which can be politically difficult; shift the burden of spending to the private sector, which makes business uncompetitive; or shift the tax basis to consumption, though that can hit the poor disproportionately.

While the principles of the tax system mean that goals such as fairness and social aims complement economic aims, tax should be simple, clear and bring value for money. Tax should be levied on 'bads', e.g. pollution, not 'goods'; increases on 'bads' should be offset by lowering tax on 'goods'. Above all, the tax system should not be a bar to economic growth: tax on incomes should be kept low lest the taxpayer flees and fall more heavily on consumption with exemptions to reduce the burdens on less well off.

Deepak Lal considers the trend towards interdependency between the state and the taxpayer. The predatory tax-levying state tends to have taxpayers' support on account of the benefits of the welfare state. But, says Lal, that trend may now be ending: economic crises can prompt taxpayers to flee from high costs or rebel against them when public services deteriorate.

In these circumstances the right course for the state is to reform. Competition in the global economy will add to the pressure to change and curb tax and public spending levels. Global competition, Lal suggests, may allow the UK to survive and adopt the classical liberal thinking needed in economic policy.

The future of welfare?

Western countries face rising costs. Working life is less secure and ageing populations bring higher costs. Welfare systems encourage dependency, but by changing the way funds are distributed, they can continue to support the social provision which Western societies want.

Peter Birch Sørensen and *Arij Lans Bovenberg* consider the case of unemployment and other benefits for people of working age which often act as a disincentive for work. They propose that an individually owned savings account should replace these. Each taxpayer would pay a percentage of earnings (with a corresponding deduction from income tax) into the account. If no claim were made for benefit, the savings would grow. But if benefit were drawn, the account would be debited. On retirement, those in debt would draw the standard state pension to which they are entitled under the current system. Those with a surplus would be awarded a higher pension.

Such a system would meet the classic aims of social insurance and the Beveridge system – to provide liquidity insurance (cash benefits) and redistribute income over the life cycle – without the present arrangements which have created a complex system churning the funds for an individual over the life cycle ('intra personal redistribution)[1].

Individual accounts would give the same entitlements as now: out-of-work cash benefits, redistribution of lifetime income and protection of those who would not otherwise save. It would also counter the present problem of disincentive ('moral hazard') by rewarding work, while protecting those in real poverty and those with a negative balance on their accounts, and cutting bureaucratic 'churning' .

Dennis Snower and Alessio Brown suggest a personal accounts model could be applied to other benefits such as health, education or pensions. They explain that as matters stand the welfare system is inefficient and unresponsive, and lacks any means to change itself or behaviour. Benefit accounts for one third of all government spending, but people cannot use the asset unless they fulfil the conditions, e.g. unemployment. A fresh direction is needed so that the system itself is more efficient and people can own their own accounts and have greater incentive to work and save.

One of the fundamental problems is that the welfare system has no competition or price mechanism to reflect demand and provides no encouragement for new suppliers to compete. Governments have 'soft' budget constraints since they find the money from tax. Costs can be high without competition. Under a system of individually owned welfare accounts people would own their funds and have the incentive not to waste them. Accounts could be created for other benefits, e.g. education and training, health and retirement, and at the end of working life balances could be used to top up pensions. The introduction of such accounts, run on a PAYG basis initially, but eventually fully funded, could be self-financing. The estimates for France, Germany and Italy suggest a cut in unemployment rates of 50 per cent, 36 per cent and 34 per cent respectively.

---

[1] 60-70% of income in the UK is redistributed to the individual over a lifetime.

I
Taxing Trends:
The Economic Role of the State

Vito Tanzi

Introduction

This chapter will consider and identify developments which affected taxation in Western industrial countries over the past century. It will explore the influence of supply and demand on tax levels, and the proportion of revenue raised. What was the interaction with public spending? How far were tax trends affected by the changing political, economic, social and cultural contexts of the time? The trends in, and factors governing, taxation will be considered from a longer-term perspective in four separate periods: before World War One; between World War One and around 1960; the four decades after 1960; and the 21st century. Though the distinction between the periods is not clear-cut and there is overlapping, nonetheless the separation of the periods allows some conclusions to emerge.

The chapter will also address the forces set to influence the future direction of tax, and analyse the pressures both to increase revenue and to curtail, or reform, taxation. It will speculate on likely future developments, focusing on industrial countries where the current average level of taxation is around 40 per cent of gross domestic product. In particular, it will consider whether the trends to higher revenue and spending over the 20th century, which reflected different priorities, will give way to a different balance in the 21st. What factors might counter increased pressure (e.g. from demographic change) for higher levels of tax and spending? What trends have already emerged which may affect the supply of, and demand for, higher levels of tax in industrial countries?

Such an analysis will help to identify the forces governing levels and types of tax, the pressures for change and the factors most likely to make for future reform.

Rising levels of tax: From laissez faire to spend and promise

At the start of the 20th century, levels of tax and public spending were anchored in the 19th century culture of low taxation, where government's role was limited to fundamental activities such as financing public works and institutions, defence, protection of individuals and property, the financing of basic education and some assistance to the very poor.

This period is often characterized as one of 'laissez-faire' where the role of the state in the economy is limited and where taxation is low-level. The spirit of the time can be captured by the statements about taxation made contemporaneously by those with specialist knowledge of the subject including Paul Leroy-Beaulieu, a public financer and scholar with extensive knowledge of fiscal developments world-wide, whose views of taxation in the late 19th century continue to be of interest to economists. He considered tax levels of 5-6 per cent of national income as 'moderate;' those of 10-12 per cent as 'heavy;' and those above 12 per cent of national incomes as 'exorbitant' and clearly damaging to growth. In the United States, economic thinking before the outbreak of the First World War reflected some of the same principles. In 1913, when the United States Congress debated the introduction of an income tax that would be applied with a one per cent basic rate and a six per cent marginal rate on the part of income that exceeded half million US dollars at 1913 prices, the then Professor of Public Finance at Harvard University stated, at Congressional hearings, that these rates were 'clearly excessive'. When the United States income tax was finally enacted, at one per cent basic rate and at a seven per cent marginal rate on the part of income over a half million dollars, the Chairman of the Ways and Means Committee in the US Congress declared that the tax 'would produce more money than the mind of man would ever conceive to spend'.[2] The introduction of the income tax in 1913 required an amendment to the US Constitution.

Much of the statistical evidence indicates that in the period before World War One, the tax burdens of major countries were generally around 10-12 per cent of national income. In this period Colbert's[3] famous statement – that the art of taxation consists of so plucking the goose to obtain the largest amount of feathers with the minimum amount of hissing – was clearly a guiding principle. A hundred years ago the main taxes used were foreign trade taxes, property taxes based on cadastral values (that is values determined administratively and based on the physical characteristics of properties), presumptive taxes on some business activities or professions, and, occasionally, local poll taxes.

---

[2] See Tanzi, 1988, p. 99
[3] Jean-Baptiste Colbert, Finance Minister of Louis XIV of France.

How could taxes be so low at that time? Didn't governments need more revenue to carry out their essential tasks? The answer is partly found in the roles that the *demand* for tax revenue and the *supply* of tax revenue played.

First, what factors mattered in shaping the demand for tax revenue? In general, governments that focused on the *fundamental* role of the state, as outlined in 1776 by Adam Smith in *The Wealth of Nations*, did not need a lot of money and would not, even today, need much money. The role was limited to the financing of public works and public institutions, the defence of the country, the protection of individuals and property, the financing of basic education and similar activities. These were all activities related to the allocation of resources. The government's role at that time did not include attempts at stabilising the economy or at redistributing income between different categories of individuals, across individuals at different income levels, or across generations. However, it did include some resources for assisting the very poor, a role long recognised by various governments and by Adam Smith.

Table 1: Social Transfers as a Percentage of GDP at Current Prices in Select OECD Countries, 1880 to 1995

Country	1880[a]	1890[a]	1900[a]	1910[a]	1920[a]	1930[a]	1960[b]	1970[b]	1980[c]	1980[c]	1995[c]
Australia	0	0	0	1.12	1.66	2.11	7.39	7.37	12.79	10.90	14.84
Austria	0	0	0	0	0	1.20	15.88	18.90	23.27	23.43	21.39
Belgium	0.17	0.22	0.26	0.43	0.52	0.56	13.14	19.26	30.38	22.45	27.13
Canada	0	0	0	0	0.06	0.31	9.12	11.80	14.96	12.90	18.09
Denmark	0.96	1.11	1.41	1.75	2.71	3.11	12.26	19.13	27.45	26.44	30.86
Finland	0.66	0.76	0.78	0.90	0.85	2.97	8.81	13.56	19.19	18.32	31.65
France	0.46	0.54	0.57	0.81	0.64	1.05	13.42	16.68	22.55	22.95	26.93
Germany	0.50	0.53	0.59			4.82	18.10	19.53	25.66	20.42	24.92
Greece	0	0	0	0	0	0.07	10.44	9.03	11.06	8.67	14.43
Ireland						3.74	8.70	11.89	19.19	16.20	18.30
Italy	0	0	0	0	0	0.08	13.10	16.94	21.24	17.10	23.71
Japan	0.05	0.11	0.17	0.18	0.18	0.21	4.05	5.72	11.94	10.48	12.24
Netherlands	0.29	0.30	0.39	0.39	0.99	1.03	11.70	22.45	28.34	26.94	25.70
New Zealand	0.17	0.39	1.09	1.35	1.84	2.43	10.37	9.22	15.22	16.22	18.64
Norway	1.07	0.95	1.24	1.18	1.09	2.39	7.85	16.13	20.99	18.50	27.50
Sweden	0.72	0.85	0.85	1.03	1.14	2.59	10.83	16.76	25.94	12.97	19.01
Switzerland	...	...	...	...	...	1.17	4.92	8.49	14.33	...	18.87
UK	0.86	0.83	1.0	1.38	1.39	2.24	10.21	13.20	16.42	11.43	13.67
United States	0.29	0.45	0.55	0.56	0.70	0.56	7.26	10.38	15.03	21.36	22.52

Source: Lindert (2002); OECD (1985).
0 = known to be zero. Blank = not yet a sovereign state. ... = known to be positive, but number is not available.
[a] Welfare, unemployment, pensions, health, and housing subsidies.
[b] OECD old series.
[c] OECD new series

There were almost no 'social transfers' – government expenditures (in cash or in kind) that aimed to protect citizens against particular risks such as illnesses, old age, unemployment, invalidity, illiteracy and poverty. Such transfers did not exist or were very small until the second half of the last century – for welfare, unemployment compensation, pensions, health, housing subsidies and so on. These social transfers acquired some importance only in the 1930s, as Table 1 indicates, partly because of the Great Depression and partly reflecting changing attitudes about what the role of the state in the economy should be. In the period before World War One the main need for *higher* revenue came from occasional wars and (after the wars) from the need to service the public debt that had been accumulated during the wars.

One factor that would lead to demands for higher public spending, and thus higher taxes, was universal suffrage. In the United Kingdom, for example, the percentage of household heads who had voting rights rose from 4.2 in 1867 to 74.2 in 1911 and to higher levels later.[4] As Lindert put it: 'There was so little social spending of any kind before the twentieth century primarily because political voice was so restricted'.[5] The Italian economist, De Viti De Marco, influential a century ago, had already worried that universal suffrage, in societies with uneven income distributions, would lead the poorer majority to demand policies that would exploit the richer few. The masses would legislate for programmes that would benefit them while the cost would be borne by the rich.[6] The Italian edition of this book was published in the late 19th century. Later this preoccupation led some major exponents of the public choice school of economics, which developed in the 1960s and 1970s, and economists such as James Buchanan, Francesco Forte and others, to advocate constitutional limits to taxation, such as are found in the Swiss Constitution. In Buchanan's view, these limits were needed to constrain populist actions on the part of governments that could damage economic activities and limit individual freedom.[7]

Let us turn now to supply considerations and the factors that shaped the supply of revenue. Even if in this pre-World War One environment the demand for public spending had been higher, it might not have led to significantly higher tax revenue because of the difficulties that existed at that time in raising taxes. The difficulties were several: first, the middle class was

---

[4] See Lindert, 2002, p.191
[5] Lindert,2002, p.190
[6] See De Viti De Marco, 1936
[7] The leaders of the public choice school were James Buchanan and Gordon Tullock in the USA, Alan Peacock in the UK and a few others. The school was indirectly influenced by the Italian Scienza delle Finanze of a century ago. Its first journal was *Public Choice*.

still small and the taxation of the larger poor classes would have given little revenue while the taxation of the rich would have been politically difficult because they still controlled the political decisions. Second, the structure of the economy imposed strong limitations on tax collection. For example, the share of formal wages and salaries in national income was low; large establishments, capable of withholding taxes at source on incomes paid by them, or on their sales, were still few; the share of agriculture in the economy was high; and informal activities predominated. These characteristics would have made it difficult to raise significantly higher tax levels. Finally, the 'technology of taxation' was still at a rudimentary stage. The major revenue producers of future years (the global income tax, social security contributions, and the value added tax) were still unknown. Instead, import duties, rudimentary taxes on business activities, some taxes on properties, some excise taxes, and some poll taxes predominated. In spite of these limitations the United Kingdom doubled its tax burden during World War One but to levels still sharply lower than today's.

Before the outbreak of World War One, several countries introduced *national* income taxes including the United States, France, and Germany. The United Kingdom already had income taxes levied at low rates, but it increased the importance of these taxes in this period. In the United Kingdom the income tax had been introduced more than a century earlier, during the war against Napoleon. For the countries that entered World War One, the conflict provided a political opportunity, a 'cover', for those politicians that wanted to raise the level of taxation permanently. Several governments took advantage of this opportunity.

From World War One to the 1960s
During, and after, the two world wars levels of tax increased. Until 1960 the increase was not dramatic, with the tax to GDP ratio around 30 per cent of GDP in most industrial countries until the 1960s. A number of influences can be detected during this period such as changing views of the role of the state in the economy, the impact of universal suffrage, the impact of two world wars, and the changes to the structure of economies which facilitated tax collection (including the growing share of wages in national income, systems for retaining tax at source, and technological factors).

This period saw a significant increase in the level of taxation especially during World War One followed by a slow growth until World War Two when taxes were increased again to finance the war. However, from the end of World War One until about 1960 there was relatively little increase. Until 1960 taxes remained relatively low compared with the levels that they would reach a couple decades later. Between 1913 and 1960 most of the tax increase came during the wars. Taxes were still only 11 per cent of GDP in 1925-29 in the United States; 20 per cent in France in 1924-25; less than 10 per cent up to 1930, and still below 20 per cent up to 1950, in Sweden. They were about 25 per cent of GDP in 1924-25 and around 30 per cent of GDP in the early 1960s in the United Kingdom. Until the early 1960s, the tax to GDP ratio was under or near 30 per cent of GDP in most industrial countries.

The reasons for the tax increases were several:

(i) Views about the role of the state in the economy changed. Various theoretical concepts developed by economists over the years helped justify the larger spending role of the state and the need for higher taxes.[8]

(ii) By this time universal (or almost universal) suffrage had given voice to a large part of the *poorer* population, giving some substance to De Viti De Marco's worry that universal suffrage would lead the (poorer) majority to demand policies that would exploit the rich.

(iii) The impact of two world wars had allowed governments to raise tax rates with little political opposition. After the wars some of these increases had been maintained partly to service the large public debts acquired during the wars.[9]

(iv) Significant changes in the structure of the economies had facilitated tax collection. Some of these were: (a) growing shares of wages and salaries in national income (these were especially important for income taxes and social securities contributions); (b) growing importance of large firms capable of retaining taxes at source (there is some evidence that until the 1960s the 'administrative costs' of tax collection had declined); (c) significant technological breakthroughs in taxation, such as 'global' income taxes applied with highly progressive rates, and, later, the introduction of value added taxes.

In conclusion, the increase in tax levels derived from higher demands for public spending, coming from a part of the population that had acquired more political power, and a higher supply of taxes due to technological developments in taxation and structural changes in the economies.

---

[8] See Tanzi and Schuknecht, 2000
[9] Peacock and Wiseman, 1961

From the 1960s to the 1990s

During the next three decades, from the 1960s to the 1990s dramatic changes can be identified. Over the 1965-85 period the increase in tax revenue raised the share of taxes as a percentage of GDP for the European countries by about 15 percentage points - with significant tax burdens for some countries by the end of the period. The increased revenue was to come from a variety of sources and was to be facilitated by governments increasingly resorting to income taxes and by pressures on government to spend and promise.

In the first two decades after World War Two, the main role in raising tax levels was played by the (personal) global income tax. This tax was an ideal instrument for the time and came to be seen by many policy-makers and tax experts as a 'dream tax'. In the United States, 90 per cent of taxpayers had considered the income tax as a fair tax during World War Two, according to survey data published by the American Enterprise Institute.[10]

Until the 1970s several countries (including the United States and the United Kingdom) had top, marginal tax rates that at times exceeded 90 per cent. These high tax rates even inspired a Beatles' song, *The Taxman*. The lyrics of the song went: 'I shall tell you how it will be, one for you, nineteen for me, cause I am the taxman'. The song was composed in 1966 when the top marginal tax rate in the United Kingdom was 95 per cent! In the United States the marginal tax rate had been lowered, from 91 per cent in 1963 to 70 per cent in 1965-67, by the Kennedy Administration. (These rates do not include those imposed by local governments (states and counties)).

The personal income tax, applied with highly progressive rates, was seen to have many virtues: (a) because it was 'income elastic', it automatically provided a growing share of revenue over the years accompanying the growth of nominal income; (b) it was assumed to reflect the 'ability to pay' of taxpayers because of its progressivity; (c) it could be made as progressive as policy-makers desired; (d) it was an ideal instrument for social engineering, in a world that was seen to be full of 'merit goods', that is of goods the consumption of which deserved to be subsidised by the government; (e) it could be fitted (or tailor-made) to the specific circumstances of individuals or families.

With the manipulation of income taxes, tax administrations could be made to administer, indirectly, social policies through 'tax expenditures' which complemented, and at times replaced, explicit public expenditures.

---

[10] American Enterprise Institute, 2005.

Authoritatively acknowledged as 'a government spending in the form of a loss or deferment of tax revenue...' these tax expenditures can be a direct substitute for direct public spending.[11] At least 10 OECD countries, including six of the seven G-7 countries, publish tax expenditure budgets that estimate the revenue losses to the governments that are caused by these tax expenditures. Thus tax administrations became almost social ministries. At that time the income tax was seen to have two other important virtues: it had counter-cyclical power, at a time when business cycles were still a major preoccupation of policy-makers; and it was considered an efficient tax because most economists dismissed its potential negative effects on work effort and incentives. Few academic articles, if any, dealt with these potential disincentives.[12] Furthermore, though it now seems strange, books on income taxation did not even mention 'tax evasion' or 'the underground economy' as potential problems associated with income taxes.[13]

By the 1960s there was political and intellectual pressure on governments to increase public spending and to find the tax revenue to finance it.[14] Politically the climate had been changed by the popularity of the Keynesian Revolution and the call for a mixed economy. Economists and politicians convinced the public that government could efficiently improve people's lives. Public spending had become popular and attractive to politicians who could win elections by proposing new government programmes. By 1965, tax revenue as a share of GDP had grown to an average of 28 per cent for 15 countries which are now members of the European Union and 26 per cent for the OECD countries. Several European countries—France, Germany, UK, Austria, Belgium, Finland, Netherlands, and Sweden—had by this time tax levels that exceeded 30 per cent of GDP. The highest tax burden in 1965 was found in Sweden (35 per cent of GDP), followed by France (34.5 per cent of GDP) and Austria (33.9 per cent of GDP). In Sweden, between 1950 and 1965 the share of taxes into GDP had risen by more than 15 percentage points. It would increase even more in the following two decades, thereby changing completely the fiscal and social landscape of Sweden. The period between 1960 and 1985 witnessed the fastest increase in public spending and in tax levels and the establishment of mature welfare states in several countries. The growth in spending often even exceeded the growth in taxes thus leading to increases in public debts that would cause macroeconomic difficulties in later years.

---

[11] See Van den Ende, Haberham, and den Boogert, 2004
[12] See Tanzi, 1988b.
[13] See for examples, Musgrave 1959, Pechman 1971, and Goode 1964
[14] See Tanzi, 2004.

Table 2: Value Added Taxes

Countries	Date VAT Introduced	Standard Rate In 2005	Other Positive Rates	VAT Revenue (%) of GDP in 2001
Australia	2000	10.0		
Austria	1973	20.0	10; 16	8.5
Belgium	1971	21.0	6; 12	6.9
Canada	1991	7.0		2.6
Denmark	1967	25.0		9.7
Finland	1994	22.0	8; 17	8.4
France	1948	19.6	2.1; 5.5	7.8
Germany	1968	16.0	7	6.9
Greece	1987	18.0	4.8	7.5
Hungary	1988	25.0	5; 15	8.1
Iceland	1990	24.5	14	9.9
Ireland	1972	21.0	4.3; 13.5	7.2
Italy	1973	20.0	4; 10	5.4
Japan	1989	5.0		2.6
Korea	1997	10.0		4.6
Luxembourg	1970	15.0	3; 6; 12	5.8
Netherlands	1969	19.0	6	6.9
New Zealand	1986	12.5		?
Norway	1970	24.0	12	8.9
Portugal	1986	19.0	5; 12	8.0
Spain	1986	16.0	4; 7	6.2
Sweden	1969	25.0	6; 12	7.2
Switzerland	1995	7.6	2.4; 3.6	3.9
United Kingdom	1973	17.5	5	6.8
Source: International Bureau of Fiscal Documentation				

The increases in tax revenue in the period *after* 1965 came from three main sources:

(a) Between 1965 and 1985, the introduction of value-added taxes would contribute about 4 per cent of GDP in *additional* revenue in the 15 European Union countries. (See Table 2 for the year of introduction of VATs and for the 2005 rates.)

(b) The growth in social security 'contributions'. These taxes would contribute, on average, about 6 per cent of GDP in additional revenue in the 1965-85 period. The growth of these taxes would come from the rise in tax rates on the share of wages subject to tax, from the increase in the share of wages subject to taxes, and from the rise in the shares of wages and salaries in national income that was taking place at that time.

(c) The impact on tax revenue that came from increases in real incomes and in *prices*, both of which were growing rapidly until the oil crisis of 1974. This automatic increase in tax revenue was called the 'fiscal drag'. It became important especially during the inflationary years of the 1970s when it provided governments with additional revenue without the need for legislation. Income taxes (on both individuals and enterprises) would contribute about 5 per cent of GDP in *additional* revenues in the 1965-85 period. The 'fiscal drag' would in time generate interest and demands for the indexation of tax brackets for inflation to remove its effect.[15]

On average the three sources mentioned above raised the share of taxes as a proportion of GDP, for the European countries, by about 15 percentage points over the 1965-85 period. Almost the whole increase in tax levels was accounted for by these three factors. This increase helped finance the increase in social spending taking place in this period.

By the end of this period, two countries, Sweden and Denmark, had tax burdens that exceeded 50 per cent of GDP. Sweden's would reach records of 53.3 per cent of GDP in 1987 and 53.9 per cent of GDP in 2000. These were probably the highest tax burdens ever recorded in the history of the world.

The reaction against high taxes: From the 1980s to the new millennium

Whereas there had been, in the 1950s and1960s, little intellectual or political opposition to higher taxation and pressure for increased public spending, that began to change in the 1970s. Instead of increases in tax being seen as both necessary and desirable, criticism from both economists and politicians became louder over the decade, prompted by new evidence about the economic consequences of high tax rates and by the increasing reaction against complexity and instability of tax systems.

First, what came to be called 'second generation econometric models'[16] started to find significant negative effects on economic activity caused by high tax rates, effects that had been missed by earlier studies that had used less sophisticated techniques. Some of these new studies found significant disincentive effects on work, on savings, on risk-taking, and on resource allocation in general. Participation in the labour market, especially by married women and secondary workers in families, was seen to be discouraged by high tax rates.

---

[15] See Tanzi 1980.
[16] See, for example, Boskin, 1978

Second, economists and policy-makers woke up to the existence of phenomena that had probably existed before but had been missed, and had become more intense because of the higher tax rates and thus more difficult to miss. Tax evasion and especially underground (or irregular, or black) economic activities started to attract increasing attention. Rather than being fair and efficient, income taxes came to be seen as unfair and growth-retarding.

Third, and especially in the United States, this period witnessed the beginning of what came to be called the 'supply-side revolution', a revolution in economic thinking that reminded economists of the role of the supply side of the economy in economic growth. This was a reaction to the excessive and almost exclusive attention that had been paid to the demand side as a result of the popularity of Keynesian economics. Many economists started to blame high taxes for the slow growth of economies including Robert Mundell, who went on to win the Nobel prize later and was considered to be the intellectual godfather of the low-tax movement.[17] Coming in a period when growth rates had fallen, in part as a consequence of the oil crisis and of the inflation that had accompanied it, this was seen as a major flaw in the prevailing tax policies. The so-called 'Laffer curve' added a political and popular dimension to this debate by arguing that high tax rates might even reduce tax revenue. Although some of the claims made by supply-siders may have been exaggerated, their arguments helped change perceptions about the impact of high marginal tax rates.

Finally, the emergence of two articulate and forceful leaders gave a strong political voice to this new view of the role of taxation. Mrs Thatcher and President Reagan felt strongly that the economic liberty of citizens had been much reduced by the high levels of taxation and by the increasing use of 'tax expenditures'. They spoke forcefully in favour of simplification of tax systems and of tax reductions. Margaret Thatcher had a background in tax law while Ronald Reagan was largely driven by his conservative instincts.

Thatcher and Reagan were successful in changing attitudes and had some successes in the UK and the United States in reducing *marginal* tax rates and, to a lesser extent, in widening tax bases. This move was imitated by several other countries whose political leaders were influenced by the British and American leaderships.[18] Unfortunately, Thatcher and Reagan were not able to reduce the level of public spending permanently. Fiscal deficits widened and the pressure to raise taxes reappeared. The 'starve the beast' approach to reducing public

---

[17] See, for example, the two contemporaneous discussions on the negative impact of tax by Wanniski, 1978 and Gilder, 1981.
[18] See Tanzi, 1988a

sector activities did not give immediately the desired results. Strong lobbies made it difficult for governments to cut spending. Furthermore, some of the changes in terms of tax simplification, aimed at removing the government from many economic decisions, did not prove durable. They were reversed when new governments came into power. These later governments continued to be pressured by their supporters to provide tax preferences (i.e. 'tax expenditures') for particular groups or activities. Some did not resist these pressures. This clearly occurred during the Clinton administration in the United States during which public spending was contained, but tax expenditures went up sharply. The implications of such policy for the freedom of individuals who experienced sharp reductions in their disposable income provoked taxpayers and led to a series of public criticisms from officials, advisers and politicians across the industrial countries.

Aftermath and change
The growing tax burden, its complexity, instability and inefficiency, and the absence of fiscal coherence, began to prompt popular and official rejection in the early years of the 21st century. The prevailing tax systems reduced the liberty of the citizen not only through the high tax levels (that reduced their disposable, after-tax incomes) but also through the reduction in their freedom to use their after-tax income as they wished. 'Tax expenditures' pushed individuals in the directions desired by the government, but not necessarily wanted by the citizens themselves: their spending choices differed from those they would have made in the absence of the incentives provided by the tax expenditures. For example by 2006 in the United States there were 16 tax breaks (i.e., tax incentives) for education and 26 for energy.[19]

From around 1980, the annoyance of taxpayers worldwide was directed with increasing intensity not only at the high-tax levels but also at the *complexity* and *instability* of the tax systems. This annoyance became a major factor in the changing attitude of citizens towards taxation registered in many countries in that period. In addition therefore to the level of taxation, such issues as complexity, instability, and fairness of the tax systems became important in many countries as the following examples indicate.

In Britain, instability, inefficiency, and absence of fiscal coherence characterised the tax system:[20]

> No one would design such a system on purpose and nobody did. Only a historical explanation of how it came about can be offered as justification.

---

[19] See Edwards, Chris, 2006.
[20] See Steinmo, 1993, p. 48

That is not a justification, but a demonstration of how seemingly individually rational decisions can have absurd effects in aggregate.[21]

But the British tax system is not alone in its complexity and other countries, even those with low tax levels, also suffer from complexity. It is generally the case that most tax systems have become much more complex in recent decades.

New Zealand, where reform two decades earlier aimed at simplifying the tax system and simplifying the language of laws provided a model for greater fiscal responsibility and transparency of the government's fiscal policy, had lost its way. The New Zealand Tax Code according to a 2001 report to ministers instilled 'anger, frustration, confusion, alienation'.[22]

Italy too has a problematic tax system. Some years ago the President of Italy, Eugenio Scalfaro, stated publicly that the income tax declaration that Italian taxpayers were required to fill could only have been 'designed by lunatics'. Italians take advantage of tax amnesties when they can, not because they have evaded taxes, but because they are never sure whether they have succeeded in complying with all the complex rules and requirements of the Italian laws. By paying a penalty for a violation that they may *not* have committed, they eliminate the risk and the worries of being audited and penalized at some future date.

The US system, despite being comparatively moderate in the amount of revenue it generates, is also seen complex and confusing. The National Taxpayer Advocate's *Annual Report to Congress 2005* stated (in its IRS News Release) that

> Our tax code has grown so complex that it creates opportunities for taxpayers to make inadvertent mistakes as well as to game the system…As taxpayers become confused and make mistakes, or deliberately push the envelope, the IRS understandably responds with increased enforcement actions. The exploitation of 'loopholes' leads to calls for new legislation to crack down on abuses, which in turn makes the tax laws more complex. Thus begins an endless cycle—complexity drives inadvertent error and fraud, which drive enforcement or new legislation, which drives additional complexity. In short *complexity_begets more complexity*. This cycle can only be broken by true tax simplification, followed by ongoing legislative and administrative discipline to avoid complexity creep.

---

[21] Kay and King, 1978 p. 1
[22] 'Flat-tax revolution', *The Economist*, April 16, 2005

The problems have more recently been highlighted by a Report to the President of the United States on tax reform, *Simple, Fair and Pro-Growth: Proposals to Fix America's Tax System*, prepared by the President's Advisory Panel on Federal Tax Reform (November 2005). The Report suggests that legislators have lost sight of the fact that the fundamental purpose of the tax system is to finance public spending. Other goals have distracted the system from its fundamental purpose. Second, it suggests that tax preferences replace citizens' choices with government choices and thus reduce economic freedom. Third, it indicates that 'tax preferences complicate the system, create instability, impose large compliance costs and can lead to inefficient use of resources'.

The system discourages saving and investment while leading to huge compliance costs, according to N. Gregory Mankiw writing when Chairman of the Council of Economic Advisers:

> The current tax code is a drag on the economy, discouraging saving and investment, and requiring individuals and businesses to spend billions of dollars and millions of hours each year to comply with the system...our tax system is a complicated mess... A simpler tax code would lower compliance costs...[23]

An American survey of taxpayers reported that citizens prefer 'root canal surgery' to an audit by the Internal Revenue Service and that 86 per cent consider the tax system very complex (50 per cent) or somewhat complex (36 per cent). The remaining 14 per cent probably do not pay taxes.

The complexity of the system is vividly illustrated by the dramatic expansion of pages of federal tax rules.[24] Table 3, adapted from this article, shows that when the US Federal Income Tax was introduced in 1913, there were 400 pages of federal tax rules. By 1939, the pages had increased marginally to 504. By 2006 the number of pages had grown to an extraordinary 66,498. 26,000 pages had been added just *in the past decade!* These are extraordinary figures that perhaps better than anything else show the extent to which taxes have become too complex. The attempts to create tailor-made tax systems have led to this complexity.

---

[23]Mankiw, 2004 p. 1
[24] See Edwards, 2006.

Table 3: U.S.A. Number of Pages of Federal Tax Rules, 1913-2006

Year	Number of Pages
1913	400
1939	504
1945	8,200
1954	14,000
1974	19,500
1984	26,300
1995	40,500
2006	66,498
Source: Compiled by Chris Edwards (2006) from different official sources.	

One consequence of the increasing complexity is the growth of compliance costs over the past decade even when the level of taxation may have stopped growing. Edwards reports that compliance costs rose from $112 billion in 1995 to $265 billion in 2005 while the number of forms that taxpayers may need to file reached the extraordinary number of 582 in 2006. Americans spent 6.4 billion hours on tax compliance in 2005 and 61 per cent of them used paid tax preparers. H & R Block alone, the major private tax preparer, received $2.2 billion in payments in 2005.

These costs include:

(i) Financial costs paid by individuals to tax advisers (accountants, tax lawyers, etc.);

(ii) Number of hours spent collecting information, organising it, filling the forms, and so on;

(iii) Reporting requirements for businesses, a cost that has been growing a lot in recent years;

(iv) The cost to business enterprises of having on their staff tax lawyers and accountants. This cost is often very high, especially for small enterprises. In many businesses more resources may now go towards 'tax planning' than towards developing new products or reducing the costs of production. The locations where businesses are established are more and more guided by tax considerations rather than by purely economic considerations. In many enterprises tax advisers have become more important than production engineers;

(v) Costs related to uncertainty: uncertainty as to whether the requirements imposed by the laws have been fulfilled; and uncertainty about the future course of the tax system. Predicting future tax development is becoming as important as predicting future interest rates;

(vi) Finally, the large costs to society when some of its most able individuals choose to become tax lawyers or tax accountants rather than go into more socially productive careers.

The complexity is not limited to industrial countries. For example a recent report on Brazil, published by the International Finance Corporation, *Doing Business in Brazil* (2006), states that 'The Brazilian tax system is among the most complex and burdensome in the world' and that 'Accountants estimate it would take 2600 hours for (a) firm to comply with all tax requirements – the longest in the world'.[25] In Brazil constitutional lawyers have become largely tax lawyers because of the frequency with which tax cases end up before the Constitutional Court. The same has been happening in Mexico where more than 90 per cent of all cases that end up in the Constitutional Court are tax cases.

What will govern future taxation?

One of the great issues facing Western economies is the level and type of tax for the future. Despite the picture of growing opposition to high taxes in most countries, nonetheless the levels of taxation and the complexity of the systems continued to grow through the 1990s even though the rate of growth in tax levels was much reduced from earlier decades. Is there any hope that the future will bring lower tax burdens and simpler tax systems? What will be the main influences in future years on tax systems? The two questions will be addressed next in the order in which they have been posed.

Pressures for tax reductions.
In the first years of the new century, pressures for tax reduction have become more intense. If 2000 is taken as the starting year, in the next 3-4 years – in 2003 or 2004 – several countries reduced taxes as a share of GDP, some of them significantly. These countries include Canada, the United States, Japan, Finland, France, Germany, Greece, Ireland, Italy, the Netherlands, and Sweden (see Table 4)

Table 4 allows a simple experiment. The highest levels of taxation reached in the recent past for the countries in the table can be averaged as shares of GDP. This is an average of tax levels in *different* years. Comparing this average with

---

[25] p. 9

the average of the tax levels in 2003, or the preliminary results for 2004, it can be seen that in the most recent year for which data are available (2003 or 2004), the average tax level was 2.2 per cent of GDP *below* the average of the highest levels. In some countries the fall in the level of taxation was 3 per cent of GDP or higher (US, Japan, Finland and Sweden). In New Zealand and the Netherlands, the fall was 2.9 and 2.4 per cent of GDP respectively. Some reductions in these years are also observed in the taxes on the wages of workers receiving average wages.[26] These reductions may represent temporary factors but, because many of these countries were running large fiscal deficits, the fall is likely to represent more permanent forces at work.

While the high levels of taxation begin to be reduced, some other developments, that in *time might lead to tax simplification and further tax reductions*, can be observed.

Table 4 Total Tax Revenue, 1965, 2003-2004

Country	1965	Highest Level Year reached in brackets		2003[a]	2004[p]
Canada	25.6	36.7	(1998)	33.8	33.0
U.S.A.	24.7	29.9	(2000)	25.6	25.4
Australia	21.7	32.1	(2000)	31.6	n.a. 31.6[a]
Japan	18.2	29.9	(1989)	25.3	n.a. 25.3[a]
New Zealand	24.0	38.3	(1989)	34.9	35.4
Austria	33.9	44.8	(2001)	43.1	42.9
Belgium	31.1	46.2	(2002)	45.4	45.6
Denmark	29.2	50.5	(1999)	48.3	49.6
Finland	30.4	48.0	(2000)	44.8	44.3
France	34.5	45.2	(1999)	43.4	43.7
Germany	31.6	37.4	(1977)	35.5	34.6
Greece	19.9	40.1	(1996)	35.7	n.a 35.7[a]
Ireland	24.9	37.2	(1988)	29.7	30.2
Italy	25.5	43.4	(1993)	43.1	42.2
Luxembourg	27.7	45.6	(1983)	41.3	40.6
Netherlands	32.8	45.8	(1988)	38.8	39.3
Norway	29.6	43.8	(2002)	43.4	44.9
Portugal	15.8	37.1	(2003)	37.1	n.a. 37.1[a]
Spain	14.7	34.9	(2003)	34.9	35.1
Sweden	35.0	53.9	(2000)	50.6	50.7
Switzerland	19.6	30.5	(2000)	29.5	29.4
United Kingdom	30.4	37.6	(1986)	35.6	36.1
Average	26.4	40.4	(1986)	37.8	37.8

[a] 2003 **Source:** OECD, 2005

---

[26] See OECD, 2006.

The first is the beginning of the privatisation of public pensions in several countries. The privatisation of part, or all, of public pensions started in Chile in 1981 and has spread to many countries including Australia, Argentina, Peru, Mexico, Poland, and other European countries. In the industrial countries this process is still in its infancy but, if it acquired speed and depth, it could *in time* reduce the public cost of pensions and the need to raise high taxes to finance them. It should be recalled that rising public expenditure for pensions was one of the most important factors leading to higher tax levels. Only time will tell whether this policy change can compensate for the impact on public expenditure arising from the ageing of the population. Without a significant policy change in this area, the ageing of the population can only lead to pressures for higher public spending and the need for more tax revenue.

Second, attitudes to personal income tax are changing. Over the past two decades we have seen developments that aimed to replace (a) many tax brackets and tax rates with fewer ones, and (b) highly progressive global income taxes with less progressive ones or even with what are called 'dual income taxes'.[27] The dual income taxes are essentially a return to the schedular income taxes which existed in several European countries in the first half of the last century. The dual income taxes separate from total income, incomes derived from capital investments (that are mobile), and tax them with *lower, proportional*, and *final* rates.[28]

Third, there is a movement towards 'flat-rate taxes', which have become popular in several transition economies.[29] So far they have been introduced in Estonia, Georgia, Latvia, Lithuania, Romania, Russia, Slovakia, and Ukraine and are attracting attention in other parts of the world. Some observers have linked these 'flat-rate taxes' to better economic performance. In the above mentioned countries, the rates have ranged from 12 and 13 per cent in Georgia, Ukraine and Russia, to 25, 26, and 33 per cent respectively in Latvia, Estonia and Lithuania. These are all countries without a tradition of income taxation and where the prices of assets (houses etc.) had not incorporated the effects of tax preferences given through the income tax, as has happened in industrial countries.

---

[27] For discussions of changes in income taxes over the past couple of decades see: Zee, 2004; Tanzi, 1987, OECD, Committee on Fiscal Affairs, 2005

[28] See Sørensen, 1994 and Broadway, 2005. This movement represents a major challenge to the concept of the progressive, global income tax that became popular after World War Two. The classic text on the global income tax is *Personal Income Tax* by Simons, 1938.

[29] Usefully described in *The Economist*'s cover story, April 16th, 2005

'Flat-rate' taxation leads to the replacement of multiple rates (and brackets) by essentially two: one zero-rate, for the part of gross income that is exempted, and one positive rate, for the part, above the exemption, that is taxed. Many observers seem to believe that the simplification comes from the reduction in the number of rates. However, this is a misunderstanding because a single rate can co-exist with a lot of special treatments and 'tax expenditures' while multiple rates can co-exist with a simple, comprehensive tax base. In the United States, for example, the reduction in the number of rates and brackets that came with the 1986 Reagan tax reform did not prevent the income tax from becoming much more complex in later years, as was shown earlier.

Another widespread belief is that a single – or flat-rate – tax, by lowering the highest marginal rates, will eliminate requests by pressure groups for special treatment and will somehow reduce the difficulties associated with the definition of the tax base. These are the difficulties that lead to complex tax systems. However, these requests are not likely to disappear when several rates are replaced by one rate especially when that rate can be quite high (as in Estonia). A high flat-rate tax will be needed if public spending remains high and if the exempted (or zero-rated) part of a taxpayer's income is a large proportion of the total. Additionally, a high flat-rate creates a steep step between the part of income taxed at a zero rate and the part taxed at the flat rate. This steep step may encourage tax evasion for many taxpayers who see their income exceeding the exempt part.

Finally, there is a lot of misunderstanding about the virtue of reducing the rates from several to one. Still, if a flat rate is introduced, and if the difference between before tax income and taxable income is reduced only to the level of the basic exemption, this would be a major step towards simplification. By eliminating 'tax expenditures' and high tax rates, the government would reduce its interference in the decisions of the taxpayers. It remains to be seen whether industrial countries will move into that direction. So far interest in flat taxes in these countries has been limited.

A move toward *genuine* flat-rate taxes could eliminate thousands of pages from the tax codes and the regulations that accompany the tax laws. In industrial countries, it would also bring major changes in the prices of some assets and especially in the price of houses which have been affected by the existence of large tax deductions for interest payments on mortgages. Such a move would reduce the need for tax advisers. It is easy to predict that the flat-rate tax will face strong opposition from many groups with powerful political constituencies (tax advisers, real estate agents, property owners, and so on). Some of the same forces that in past years pushed for the expansion of the role of the state in the economy would oppose the reduction of tax rates and the simplification of the tax system. Tax 'expenditures' have created powerful lobbies behind them just as government expenditures have done. In the United States the Report of the President's Advisory Panel on Federal Tax Reform quickly disappeared from the political screen once the lobbies started voicing their opposition to tax simplification that would hurt their interests.

Supply and Demand: The framework for future tax. A number of forces have already emerged to change the balance of tax and determine revenue supply. The influences on levels of taxation in future years will be considered in this section. As in the past, the final outcome in terms of future tax levels will be determined by forces that influence the demand for, and the supply of, tax revenue.

Let us start with the forces that push for more tax revenue. The ageing of the population and the impact of this phenomenon on public spending under current programmes are obvious forces that have received a lot of attention. As is well known, under current policies, demographic changes could lead to large increases in public spending for pensions, public health services, and the care of the very old. The public accounts of many countries are already in a precarious condition even though the full impact of ageing has not yet been felt. Various studies indicate that in some countries the increase in public spending under current policies could be dramatic and could easily exceed the public resources available. More public spending would of course create pressure for more tax revenue.

Over the longer run it may be possible for the government to shift its main role from a spending to a regulatory one. In recent papers, I have argued that a more sophisticated private market with some intelligent regulation and better focused public assistance could provide, for many taxpayers, the required protection against events (old age, illnesses, illiteracy, etc.) that are, to some extent, predictable. Instead of 'buying' this protection from the public sector, through the payment of taxes, the citizens would buy it from the private market against the payment of insurance fees. The lower tax payments would leave in the citizens' pockets more income that could be used for this purpose.[30] If the government could play an efficient regulatory role, and if the market could be made more efficient, many citizens would acquire more economic freedom and the needed services or protection could be provided more efficiently by the market than they are now by the public sector, especially in some countries where public sector expenditure is notoriously

---

[30] See Tanzi, 2004 and 2005.

inefficient.[31] Whether the forces of ageing, with unchanged policies, or the forces of privatisation of protection and public services, prevail will determine whether the demand for public revenue will rise or fall in the future. The result will, to a large extent, depend on who wins the ideological battle about the role of the state in the economy and on whether the government will be able to perform an efficient regulatory role.

What about the forces that determine the supply of revenue? A country may wish to have more tax revenue but be unable to get it, or at least to get it cheaply. A few factors that may have reduced the countries' capacity for, or facility in, raising or even maintaining the current tax levels can be mentioned.[32]

First, foreign competition, globalisation, and technological developments have created what could be called 'fiscal termites' that have started to damage the foundations of fiscal systems, thus increasing the country's difficulties in raising taxes. Examples of these termites are electronic commerce, transfer prices, off-shore financial centres, complex financial instruments, growing shares of incomes earned abroad, use of electronic money and so on. All these factors will make it increasingly more difficult in the future for countries to collect taxes.[33]

Second, competition from low-tax countries such as China, India, Vietnam and others will make it difficult for high-tax countries to maintain the current levels of taxation that inevitably raise the cost of what they produce. In a world where capital has become very mobile, it will tend to be invested in lower-tax countries. Financial capital will go to places where tax rates on interest incomes, dividends, profits, and so on are lower. Also as time passes, the more able individuals (engineers, scientists, etc.) will be able to move away from countries where their incomes are highly taxed.[34]

Finally, the structure of economies is likely to change in ways that will make it more difficult to maintain high taxes. For example, many activities will be carried out by establishments that are either too small, or too global, to control. The fact that income distributions are becoming less even will mean that wages (which have been easier to tax) will fall in importance while capital incomes (which are more difficult to tax) will increase. In fact the moves towards dual income taxes or flat-rate taxes will favour capital incomes over wages thus

---

[31] See Alonso et al. 2005.
[32] Some of these have been discussed at length in other places.See Tanzi, 1995 and 2001.
[33] See especially, Tanzi, 2001.
[34] See Tanzi, 1995.

creating a downward bias for tax levels. It is difficult to predict whether the 'technology of taxation' will be able to produce innovations similar to the 'global income tax' or the 'value added tax' that could provide new tax handles for the authorities to use.

A lower tax future?

Against the pattern of rising tax rates and revenue - gradually from the 1900s to the 1960s, with more significant increases during the two world wars, and dramatically in the 1960s and 1970s - certain trends affected change. And, in the 1980s, the pattern changed again as economic, political and popular disillusion prompted reactions against high and complex levels of tax and against public spending and its consequences. These changes in tax rates and tax structures and the proportion of revenue raised have been influenced by the forces of supply and demand and by changing social, cultural, political, economic (and practical) frameworks.

For the future, though the pressures to continue increasing revenue will be strong, especially if current expenditure policies remain unchanged, there may be counter-pressures on the government to change its role and scope, allowing for lower public spending and tax. For instance, government may shift its role from a spending to a regulatory one, especially given the more sophisticated private markets which can provide social goods and services for a price. It can then better focus its support from public sources on those who need it. This would allow citizens to buy protection from the private sector rather than the public sector while maintaining a government role in this area.

Other forces have already emerged to curb tax increases: foreign competition, globalisation and technological developments. These have led to the creation of 'fiscal termites' that create increasing difficulties for tax administrators (e.g. electronic commerce, transfer prices, offshore financial centres, incomes earned abroad, electronic money). In addition, competition from low-tax countries (e.g. China, India, Vietnam and others), will make it difficult for higher-tax countries to keep up present levels of expenditure, let alone increase them. Such competition may also lead to lower levels of simpler taxes in higher tax and spending countries.

This means that there is, for the future, the prospect of a world in which the level of taxation is lower, the taxes are simpler, and the state plays a less intrusive and more efficient role in the economy. Governments should focus their activities more efficiently toward their historical, traditional role (that would include making markets function more efficiently) and markets should be allowed and encouraged to provide social services (in health, education, pensions, etc.) to the citizens. By paying less tax, the citizens would have higher after-tax incomes to purchase these services directly from the market and not through the mediation of the state. The role of the state should be to set the rules and to focus on the small group of citizens who, through no fault of their own, would not be able to buy these basic services directly from the market. This would increase the economic freedom of most individuals and reduce the weight of the state on the economy.

Tax simplification should be pursued as an important objective independently from the objective of reducing the level of taxation. It was argued earlier that tax systems have become extremely complex, burdening taxpayers not only through the tax payments they make but also through the requirements on how to estimate and pay what they owe the state. Governments will rediscover that the objective of taxation is to provide revenues for the state to meet its obligations and not to engage in social engineering through the tax system.

Bibliography

Advisory Panel on Federal Tax Reform, (USA), *Simple, Fair and Pro-Growth: Proposals to Fix America's Tax System,* Washington DC, 2005.

Afonso, A., L. Schuknecht, and V. Tanzi, 'Public Sector Efficiency: An International Comparison', *Public Choice 123,* 2005, pp.321-347.

American Enterprise Institute, *Taxpayers Surveys,* Washington DC, 2005.

Boadway, R., 'Income Tax Reform for a Globalized World: The Case for a Dual Income Tax', in *Journal of Asian Economics,* 16, 2005 pp.910-927.

Boskin, M., 'Taxation, Saving and the Rate of Interest', *Journal of Political Economy,* 86, 1978, p.2.

De Viti De Marco, A., *First Principles of Public Finance,* London, 1936.

Edwards, C., 'Income Tax Rife with Complexity and Inefficiency,' in *Tax and Budget,* Bulletin of the Cato Institute, No. 3, Washington DC, 2006.

Gilder, G., *Wealth and Poverty,* New York, 1981.

Goode, R., *The Individual Income Tax,* Washington DC, 1964.

Zee, H., 'World Trends in Tax Policy: An Economic Perspective', *Intertax,* Vol. 32, issue 8/9, 2004, pp. 352-64.

Kay, J.A. and M.A. King, *The British Tax System,* Oxford, 1978.

Leroy, Beaulieu, Paul, *Traite de la Science des Finances,* Paris, 1888.

Lindert, P.H., 'What Drives Social Spending? 1770 to 2020', in *When Market Fail: Social Policy and Economic Reform,* edited by E. B. Kapstein and B. Milanovic, New York, 2002, pp.185-214.

Mankiw, N.G., 'The Economic Agenda', *The Economists' Voice,* Vol. I, Issue 3., 2004.

Musgrave, R., *The Theory of Public Finance,* New York, 1959.

National Taxpayer Advocate U.S.A., *Report to Congress,* 2005.

OECD, *Social Expenditure*, Paris, 1985.

OECD, *Revenue Statistics*, 1965-2004, Paris, 2005.

OECD, Committee on Fiscal Affairs, *Recent Experiences of OECD Countries with Tax Reform* and *Fundamental Reform of Personal Income Tax*, Paris, 2005.

OECD, *Taxing Wages*, 2004-2005,Paris, 2006.

Peacock, A. and J. Wiseman, *The Growth of Public Expenditure in the United Kingdom*, Princeton N.J., 1961.

Pechman, J.A., *Federal Tax Policy*, New York, 1971.

President's Advisory Panel on Federal Tax Reform, *Simple, Fair, and pro-Growth: Proposals to Fix America's Tax System*, Washington DC, 2005.

Simons, H.C., *Personal Income Taxation*, Chicago, 1938.

Sørensen, P.B., 'From the Global Income Tax to the Dual Income Tax: Recent Reforms in the Nordic Countries,' *International Tax and Public Finance* 1, 1994, pp.57-79.

Steinmo, S., *Taxation and Democracy: Swedish, British and American Approaches to Financing the Modern State*, New Haven CT, 1993.

Tanzi, V., *Inflation and the Personal Income Tax; An International Perspective*, Cambridge, 1980.

Tanzi, V., 'The response of Other Industrial Countries to the US Tax Reform Act', *National Tax Journal*, Vol. XL, No. 3, 1987, pp 339-55.

Tanzi, V., 'Tax Reform in Industrial Countries and the Impact of the U.S. Tax Reform Act of 1986.' *International Bureau of Fiscal Documentation Bulletin*, Vol. 42, No. 2 (February) 1988a.

Tanzi, V., 'Trends in Tax Policy as Revealed by Recent Developments and Research', *International Bureau of Fiscal Documentations Bulletin*, Vol. 42, No. 3 (March) 1988b.

Tanzi, V., *Taxation in an Integrating World*, Washington DC, 1995.

Tanzi, V., 'Globalization, Technological Development and the Work of Fiscal Termites,' *Brooklyn Journal of International Law*, Vol. XXVI, No. 4, 2001.

Tanzi, V., *A Lower Tax Future? The Economic Role of the State in the 21st Century*, Politeia, London, 2004.

Tanzi, V., 'Role of Government and Public Spending in a Changing World,' *Rivista di Diritto Finanziario e Scienza delle Finanze*, Anno LXIV, Fasc. 3, 2005 pp. 321-339.

Tanzi, V., and L. Schuknecht, *Public Spending in the 20th Century*, Cambridge, 2000.

Van den Ende, L., A. Haberham, and K. den Boogert, *Tax Expenditure in the Netherlands* in Tax Expenditures – *Shedding Light on Government Spending through the Tax System*, edited by Hana Polachova Brixi, Christian Valenduc, and Zhicheng Li Swift, Amsterdam, 2004.

Wanniski, J., *The Way the World Works*, New York, 1978.

II
Taxes in a Global Economy:
Efficiency, Fairness and Incentives

By Irwin Stelzer

Introduction

The next government will feel compelled to raise taxes. But which taxes? Will it be able simply to follow past practices – raise taxes on 'the rich', for example, or will it be forced to resort to other instruments of policy to restore fiscal sanity while maintaining the support of Britain's voters?

My thesis is as follows. Globalisation and the increased mobility of all the factors of production have placed limits on the ability of states to impose new taxes; that has led to an attempt to eliminate tax competition. Since it will be difficult for governments to cut either domestic or defence spending, limitations on their ability to raise taxes will result in an attempt to shift the burden of the welfare state from governments to the private sector. They will also find that the desire for an efficient, growth-friendly tax structure often conflicts with voters' notions of equity.[35]

Globalisation and Tax Policy – Capital, Labour and Land:

First, a word about the effect of globalisation – a much abused word, but relevant for our purposes – on tax policy, treating in turn capital, labour, and – surprise – land.

Capital
The declining cost of communication, which now has a marginal cost close to zero, has made it possible for capital to move across borders at the touch of button, at times by some teenager posing as a sophisticated trader in currency, shares, bonds, and complicated financial instruments, at other times by long-term investors such as Warren Buffett, a man whose interests are hardly as parochial as his personal habits might suggest. At times, senior management is aware of what is going on; at others, so effortless has it become to shift billions hither and yon, fortunes are made and lost without the sleep of grown-ups

---

[35] An interesting discussion of the roles of efficiency and equity in policy-making can be found in Ed Balls, Joe Grice and Gus O'Donnell (eds.), 2004, pp.333-340.

being at all disturbed. At times, capital flows into an economy in which prospects seem bright, at times it flows out, often at speeds so blinding as to cause economic upheavals. Needless to say, this capital is constantly shopping for the most benign tax environments available, other things being equal.

Labour

The situation in the case of the second factor of production, labour, is more complicated. At the highly skilled end, the market for talent is international in scope, and competition for managers capable of running international enterprises, and for those capable of creating intellectual property, is intense. In response to the intense competition for such talent we witnessed the growth of a mobile class composed of men and women who are almost indifferent to the location at which they ply their various trades – that is a bit of an exaggeration, since man does not live by champagne alone – but still basically correct. The high income these people can command gives them the wherewithal to feather a comfortable nest in almost any place in which an attractive assignment is available, and in which they find the tax climate agreeable – again, other things being equal, the traditional caveat deployed by all economists, and applicable throughout this essay.

At the other end of the labour market are workers far less mobile, but nevertheless involved in international competition, although of a somewhat different and less satisfying sort. They produce goods, and in an increasing number of cases services, that are marketed throughout the world. In effect, therefore, they compete with one another. Unlike those in the top tier of the labour market, where competition for the workers' output drives up the prices they can command, those in the bottom tier face fierce competition for the goods they produce, driving prices steadily down – and with them, wages employers can afford to pay. The entry of over one billion very low-paid Chinese workers into the international market has increased that downward pressure. The products these people produce are internationally mobile, but the producers are not. But the taxing authorities cannot find much revenue among these lowest-earning of these workers.

Unfortunately for the geese in the broad middle – less mobile than the higher earners referred to earlier – they are there for the plucking, with the result that in many countries, including the US and the UK, the tax burden has been shifted from those rich enough to flee, and those too low-paid to pay, to the broad middle class.

But even here, the authorities are running into difficulties. For one thing, increasingly overburdened middle-class taxpayers are becoming increasingly hostile voters, and with good reason: as the pressure of international competition prevents their wages from rising, any increase in their taxes reduces their real disposal income – their standard of living, in non-jargon terms. For another, an increasing number of workers in this middle class are internationally mobile – the famous 'Polish plumber'. They cannot command wages anything like the scarcer executive group, but the declining cost of transportation (Ryanair offers a £65 round-trip fare, Krakow-London) and the increased openness of borders – legal and otherwise – enable them to follow the money, and that means after-tax money. Indeed, it is not stretching a point too far to point out that in some instances even the lowest paid workers, the poor Mexicans who stream across the US border in their millions, for example, are able to seek out the best after-tax incomes on offer. This mobility has an equalising effect on wage rates, holding them down in countries to which they flock[36] – the UK and the US, for example – and driving them up in the countries that at some point need to woo them back or retain them. Recession-driven reductions in international labour flows will be reversed when recovery takes hold.

Others in this middle group are shielded from the international market, at least for the most part. Think of your dry cleaner, your barber or hairdresser and other purveyors of various services. They need worry only about competition from similarly situated workers in their own countries, although this becomes less true every day: international competition in the provision of medical services is one example of such competition that was unheard of just a few years ago.

The most thoroughly protected are public service workers: their political power, in part a result of their concentration in certain constituencies here, has so far protected them from off-shoring and from the need to increase efficiency in an internationalised labour market that drives other workers to compete. Which is why public-sector compensation (wages, benefits, pensions) is rising faster than private-sector compensation of workers performing similar tasks, despite the lower risk associated with most lifetime-tenured public sector employment.

Land
Finally we have the third factor of production: land. It is a completely immobile resource, but increasingly subject to international competition as members of the mobile executive class compare property values around the

---

[36] There is considerable controversy concerning the effect of immigration on the wages and job opportunities of the native work-force, and an extensive academic literature on the subject.

world when making their location decisions, and manufacturers consider the cost of purchasing land or paying rent when deciding where to locate their businesses. Still, land – and the houses built on land – remains a *relatively* immobile resource, which may account for the rapid rise in property taxes.

In sum, we have a world in which the factors of production are subject to varying degrees of international competition. Top executives move around the globe in search of higher after-tax pay and better lives; some workers in the middle of the income scale also find they can seek greener pastures; lower-paid workers have jobs only so long as their employers do not find greener pastures; and owners of properties find themselves at least somewhat subjected to international competition, especially at the top end of the residential market, and in the market to attract factories; only government workers are shielded – in part by the nature of their work, in part by their political power – from globalised competition. Which might explain the declining productivity in the public sector – but that is another subject.

The Limits to Tax?

We should not exaggerate, and claim that these forces completely neuter the taxing authorities. Were that so, Gordon Brown would have been unable to raise taxes steadily over the past decade, to the point where the state now claims about 43 per cent of all the income produced by the private sector. But even he recognised, at least until recently, the limitations imposed by international competition,[37] and resorted to stealth taxes[38] of the sort that are barely noticed in the short run, and do not produce tax flight.

Nor should we fall into the trap of the most devoted of the supply-siders, and assume that any tax increase will reduce the total flow of revenue to the state, or that any tax cut will have the effect of increasing tax receipts. Some tax changes will have such effects, but not all. Thus, we do not yet know whether

---

[37] 'It has certainly entered his [Brown's] soul that if taxes on individuals and companies are raised to relatively high levels by international standards, many will relocate themselves or their wealth to another country where taxes are lower.' So wrote Robert Peston only five years ago. See his *Brown's Britain*, London, 2005, p.254. Since then Brown has done some soul-searching and decided that he can risk some exodus of individuals and businesses if he raises taxes.

[38] The purpose of Brown's 'prudence' in the early years of his chancellorship 'was not so different from that of previous Labour governments: it was to invest in public services and augment the income of the poor ... In the first few years he took advantage of a growing economy and a general sense of optimism to raise revenues from new imposts in ways that weren't widely noticed ...'. Peston, 2005, pp. 248 -:

the proposed increase in the taxes extracted from foreign 'non-doms'[39] will produce the increased revenues that both Labour and the Tories predict, or cause so great an exodus of high earners who now pay taxes on UK incomes, VAT, stamp duty, and other levies, and create taxable jobs, that total receipts will decline, as some in the City expect. Most likely, since other things are never equal, since the impact of most tax changes is difficult to isolate from other factors such as changes in the level of economic activity, and since the impact is rarely felt immediately, we will never know with sufficient certainty to quell the debate on the effect of this (and other) tax changes.

But it is certainly plausible to argue that most governments have exhausted their ability to raise tax rates significantly. There are two reasons. First, governments don't like to lose elections, and although past increases in taxes have been accepted, it is not clear that further rises will not lead to massive voter dissatisfaction. I know that when asked whether they want tax cuts or more public spending, voters often say they favour the latter – lest they seem mean. That is rather like voters not telling pollsters that they plan to vote for the Tories, lest they seem ungenerous to the less well off, or – in the US – replying that they do not know which candidate they will support rather than admit they would never vote for a black.

My own impression is that there was indeed a period in which voters felt the public services were under-funded, and they might have been right, but now that their taxes have risen, and spending has increased substantially, they expect improvements to come from better management of the plentiful resources now available – a forlorn hope, since there is no significant incentive on the part of suppliers of those services to improve output. That, too, is a subject for another day.

The second reason to believe that governments are at, or close to, the limits of their ability to raise taxes is the increasing incidence of tax avoidance, the perfectly legal practice of minimising the taxes paid. Tesco's use of the Cayman Islands' low-to-no tax regime to shelter from tax the capital gains it will earn from selling and leasing back £6 billion worth of its stores is but the most recent and widely publicised example. Scores of advisers, accountants and lawyers – some of the best minds in Britain – earn their livings by devising perfectly legal avoidance methods, and by comparison shopping for advantageous tax jurisdictions with a devotion equal to the most dedicated Internet devotee of comparative shopping sites.

---

[39] Workers resident in the UK but planning to return to their native countries.

So, the competition countries such as Britain now face comes from other taxing jurisdictions, not merely from cheap labour. The local, nation-by-nation monopoly of taxing powers is breaking down. Like other monopolists who find their once-total control under threat from newcomers, high-taxing nation states' first reaction is to form a cartel, sailing under the pleasant-sounding banner 'harmonisation'. The EU wants to stop ruinous tax competition from Eastern Europe countries benefiting from low, and in some cases flat, taxes (Estonia provides the leading example of the sort of country that can benefit from a flat tax); the UK, US, and Germany are particularly upset with Liechtenstein, which offers a legal tax-effective investment climate. So effective has that tiny country (population 35,000) been in attracting capital that it has become one of the most prosperous in the world, at the same time winning approval of the Financial Action Task Force[*] and America's Internal Revenue Service for its tough line on dirty money. There is nothing a cartel hates more than a cut-price competitor, be it Liechtenstein, or Luxembourg, or Ireland with its 12.5 per cent corporate tax rate, or Monaco which combines sunshine and low taxes, making it a deadly challenger to the high-tax nations for some important activities. And there is nothing that benefits ordinary taxpayers more, and stimulates economic growth more, than the constraint imposed on greedy chancellors by competition. Carl Mortished put it beautifully in *The Times* (February 27, 2008):

> Without the competing lure of some neighbouring fiscal paradise, Europe would certainly be a tax hell, a land of disinvestment and unemployment, governed by parasitic states and funded by an overburdened and shrinking middle class. Those with long memories will recollect Britain in the 1970s when the top tax rate was close to 80 per cent.

The Options

All of this leaves government with three alternatives:

Cut spending
One way to cope with limitations on the power to tax is to curb spending, not an easy thing to do. In most countries military spending has been so reduced as to leave little room for further cutbacks. European countries spend so little on their militaries that they cannot move troops without using US-provided transport, or meet their NATO commitments in Afghanistan. British soldiers

---

[*] The Financial Action Task Force (FATF) is an inter-governmental body whose purpose is the development and promotion of national and international policies to combat money-laundering and terrorist financing.

are suffering, and in some cases dying, because the Government has failed to provide adequate funds for communications equipment, armour, and other equipment, not to mention adequate housing for families of serving soldiers.

Until now, Europeans have been able to fund their welfare states by short-changing their military establishments. That happy circumstance is about to end. As the American Secretaries of State and Defense have recently made clear in meetings with NATO allies, the US is growing impatient with the free-riding of other countries on American defence expenditures. With the Democrats in control of both Houses of Congress, and in the White House, eager to divert funds to health care and other domestic needs, the day when America will pay for the pacification of the Balkans and other areas of more concern to the Europeans is coming to an end.

This leaves the various entitlement and other welfare-state programmes as candidates for reduction. I doubt very much whether such cuts are achievable – after all, politicians even regard a slowing of the increase in spending as a reduction. In Britain, neither party will reveal just how it plans to cut spending (ignore calls for greater efficiency), in America the Democrats planned to expand spending on the young, the old, the sick, or the otherwise disadvantaged. Indeed, in most countries the ageing of the population, the marvellous but costly developments in the field of medicine, and rising consumer awareness of the benefits of expensive courses of treatment, will drive pension, health care and related costs inexorably upward.

With the scope for new taxes limited by international competition, and the scope for spending cuts limited by the already-shrunken size of military budgets and political resistance to cuts in welfare spending, governments' next alternative is to turn to the private sector.

Burden the Private Sector
I suggested earlier that governments reaching the end of their ability to raise taxes not only seek to stamp out tax competition, but also seek to shift the burden of the welfare state to the private sector. There is no need to raise taxes on pollution when government can require utilities to incur the added costs of producing or buying power from, more costly, renewable sources; there is no need to raise taxes to fund programmes to end 'fuel poverty' when the Chancellor can compel energy providers to fund such programmes with a slice of their profits; there is no need to raise taxes when the cost of 'improving workers' work-life balance' can be imposed on private companies by expanding maternity and paternity leave; there is no need to raise taxes to install devices to improve access to the workplace by the disabled when a

simple regulation imposes that cost on private companies; and there is no need to raise taxes to pay for more police when a frightened private sector installs and pays for the devices that have reduced car theft in recent years.

In America, when Ronald Reagan's fiscal deficits led us to believe that the liberals (in the American sense) would not be able to enact and fund new welfare programmes that would expand the reach of the state, we found that Congress would simply pass laws forcing private companies to implement new programmes, and bear the costs or pass them on in their prices. Voters get angry with politicians when taxes go up, but with corporations when prices go up.

This tendency to burden the private sector will, of course, in the long run reduce the international competitiveness of any nation's enterprises. But the process will be slow, and less visible to voters. Moreover, a handy way out exists for governments that choose this route – protectionism. Britain and Australia may just turn out to be the last men standing in the ranks of free traders, and even Britain is leaning in a 'Britain-first' direction when it comes to jobs and the allocation of capital. Certainly, with the honourable exception of John McCain, most politicians in America would prefer to erect trade barriers than to reduce the environmental, employment and other costs imposed by legislation on major corporations. Indeed, the trend is likely to be in the other direction. Barack Obama favours a Patriot Employer Act that would provide tax breaks for 'patriotic employers'. To join that favoured group a company must pay at least 60 per cent of each employee's health care premiums, not insist on a secret ballot in union recognition elections, increase the number of full-time workers in America relative to those it employs overseas, provide a pension plan, and pay a salary equal to or above the federal poverty level. Then there is the 'buy American' provision of the stimulus package – naked protectionism.

Shift the tax base
If governments cannot raise taxes in the conventional way very much, cannot cut military expenditures further and either cannot or will not rein in the size of their welfare states, and recognise that perpetual deficit spending eventually leads to inflation and a devaluation of the currency, they have one other choice: shift to consumption taxes. Tax jobs, and workers and job-creating investors can flee; tax profits and companies will double their efforts to avoid taxes or find more congenial business environments; tax land, and at least some projects will be located in lower-tax areas.

But tax consumption and most of these constraints are removed.[40] Yes, at some point consumers will rebel, but they are less likely to do so if taxes on what they buy go up, than if their pay packets are raided. That is why opponents of any tax increases so fear VAT – it is easier to raise than income taxes.

Yes, there will be smuggling across national or, in America, state borders of highly taxed items such as cigarettes and booze. But consumption taxes make it more attractive to save and invest than to spend on current consumption, and certainly have a less discouraging effect on the incentives to work and take risks.[41]

The problem is that consumption taxes can be regressive, since lower-income people spend proportionately more of their incomes than do their better-off counterparts, and certainly spend a higher portion on what we call 'necessities', an extraordinarily vague and elastic concept that it would tax the ingenuity of the tax collector to define. Food is the easiest example, clearly a necessity – until we realise that the shelves of any supermarket display more than what song-writer Terry Gilkyon called 'the simple bare necessities'. Children's clothing is another seemingly simple candidate for exemption from consumption taxes, until we realise that the dividing line between clothing for children and garb for adults is no longer quite as distinct as it once was.

Nevertheless, these problems seem just as soluble as that of defining income, or separating business from personal expenditures. And consumption taxes do not seem to contain the disincentive to work, and the incentives to flee from or avoid the taxman, that are often the consequence of increases in other forms of taxation.

The Underlying Principles of Taxation:

Conflicting goals of tax policy
Until now I have emphasised the limitations on tax policy created by competition from lower-tax jurisdictions. Let me conclude by citing one more limitation – perhaps more profound than even the increased mobility of most of the factors of production. I have in mind the pressure created by the three often conflicting goals of tax policy: efficiency, fairness, and the shaping of

---

[40] Milton Friedman, 1953, pp. 100-113.
[41] Taxes on interest income, for example, discourage savings whereas if 'all income that is saved would not be taxed until the saving is later spent' people's savings decisions would not be distorted. Individual retirement plans such as the 401(k) programme in America move in the direction of a consumption tax: savings deposited in these accounts escape taxation until the money is withdrawn at retirement.

society, the latter known to its critics as social engineering. And here I draw on a paper I prepared for The Smith Institute.

All systems of taxation in democratic societies are designed to accomplish three goals: efficiency, fairness, and the shaping of society. Unfortunately, these goals often pull politicians in opposite directions.

Efficiency dictates avoiding taxes that deter the most talented, hard-working, and risk-tolerant members of society from doing their utmost to add to their own and the nation's wealth. Taxes, taught Adam Smith, should not 'obstruct the industry of the people, and discourage them from applying to certain branches of business which might give maintenance and employment to great multitudes.'[42]

Efficiency also requires that taxes be levied on consumption in instances in which that consumption produces externalities that impose significant costs on others, such as the pollution caused by the consumption of fossil fuels, to take a currently prominent example. Such taxes add to the efficiency with which resources are allocated by forcing consumers to pay prices that reflect the full costs of their consumption choices, and by generating revenue that reduces the need for incentive-reducing taxes on the incomes of workers and risk-taking entrepreneurs.

In short, tax policy should encourage the optimally efficient use of the nation's human and other resources. At least, so economists would argue. But considerations of fairness often trump economics, not a bad thing in a democracy in which citizens' notions of fairness must be satisfied lest tax evasion become a national sport. Fairness, or equity, is of course, a concept of infinite elasticity. As John Selden[43] long ago noted:

> Equity is a roguish thing. For Law we have a measure, know what to trust to; equity is according to the conscience of him that is chancellor, and as that is larger or narrower, so is equity. 'Tis all one as if they should make the standard for the measure we call a foot a chancellor's foot. What an uncertain measure would this be! One chancellor has a long foot, another a short foot, a third an indifferent foot; 'Tis the same thing in the Chancellor's conscience.

---

[42] R.H. Campbell & A.S. Skinner, (general editors) W.B. Todd (textual editor), *An Inquiry Into The Nature And Causes Of The Wealth Of Nations*, Clarendon Press, Oxford, 1976, p.826.
[43] Samuel Harvey Reynolds (ed.), 1892, p.61.

In practice, the quest for fairness becomes a search for means of making *post-tax* incomes more equal than unfettered market forces make *pre-tax* incomes.[44] Different societies have different tolerance levels for inequality, but most deem it appropriate to impose some form of 'progressive' taxation on incomes – higher rates of tax on high earners than on those lower down on the income scale. They find support in Smith, who argued that those who benefit most from 'the protection of the state', as measured by their earnings, ought to pay a higher proportion of their incomes to the state.[45] Recent experience suggests that such policies at some point clash with the goal of efficiency: they raise marginal tax rates to levels that so discourage work, and/or increase the value of avoidance techniques, that the increases become counter-productive.[46] Unfortunately, we can never know in advance just what that counter-productive rate is.

This leaves us with the third objective of tax policy: what has come to be called social engineering. Some policies favour families as traditionally structured, others confer benefits on farmers in the interests of 'food security' or the preservation of the countryside, others encourage home ownership, still others favour certain technologies. The list is rather close to infinite.

With social engineering comes complexity. And with complexity a reduction in efficiency. For one thing, a complex tax code creates uncertainty: it makes investment planning more difficult, as the net after-tax proceeds of any venture will depend importantly on which of the several provisions of the complex tax code applies.

For another, complexity is costly, both to the taxpayer and the tax collector.[47] Smith warned of a tax structure that 'may require a great number of officers, whose salaries may eat up the greater part or the produce of the tax'[48] – an extreme example, perhaps, although some taxes are indeed extraordinarily costly to collect, and others to compute.

Unfortunately, both the search for equity and the desire to achieve certain social goals not only create inefficiencies – they fail to achieve their own stated

---

[44] Friedman, 1982, Chapter X, 'The Distribution of Income'.
[45] *Ibid.* p.825.
[46] Robert J. Barro argues that 'a roughly uniform tax on the broad middle class' produces fewer inefficient distortions than does a progressive tax on incomes. *Getting It Right: Markets and Choices in a Free Society*, The MIT Press, Cambridge, Mass. and London, 1996, p.126; also pp. 114-115.
[47] Mankiw, 2004, p.250.
[48] *Ibid.* p. 826.

objectives by themselves creating 'all sorts of inequities... It makes people feel that the tax system is unfair and that they are not getting their fair share of tax breaks.'[49] Encourage home ownership by allowing the deduction of mortgage interest and renters are offended; encourage the traditional family with special tax treatment and single parents are offended. The fate of social engineers often proves to be an unhappy one.

Balancing the conflicting goals of efficiency, fairness, and social engineering is difficult enough when dealing with currently earned incomes, witness the periodic furores over executive compensation, and the heated debates about whether and how tax policy should be used to narrow the income gap between high and low earners. It is even more difficult when we are dealing with wealth. The pursuit of wealth can, and does, drive people to work and take risks; in short, to seek to earn as much as they can. The income they derive from that pursuit is taxed by the state, somehow balancing the often competing demands of efficiency, equity, and social policy. That portion that the state does not seize remains in the hands of the individual – and what is not spent becomes his or her wealth, the accumulation of after-tax income that is not spent on current consumption.

It is therefore arguable that, having once passed through the tax wringer when earned, wealth should be exempt from further taxation. For it seems both unfair to double-tax this wealth, and inefficient in that such a tax might reduce incentives to accumulate wealth by working hard to maximise earnings.

Would that life were so simple. Wealth includes not only the accumulation of the proceeds of work and risk-taking, but windfalls, additions to personal wealth completely unrelated to any contribution to society. Homeowners, for example, have accumulated wealth in many countries merely by 'being there': the availability of cheap credit, constraints on the supply of housing, and other factors unrelated to the skills or effort of homeowners, have enriched them significantly.

This is not the place to resolve all of the issues surrounding taxation of all forms of wealth. That subject, too, deserves separate treatment, I will resist the temptation to repeat my already-too-often repeated defence of inheritance taxes,[50] other than to point out that Anthony Crosland was simply wrong

---

[49] Leonard Burman, 'Comment on Tax Policy', in Jeffrey Frankel and Peter Orszag (eds.)., 2002, p.180.
[50] See my 'From Grave to Cradle: Building a Meritocracy,' London, Social Market Foundation, September 2002, and articles appearing in *The Spectator*, *The Weekly Standard* and other publications.

when he wrote that one advantage of taxes on inheritances is that 'They are politically perhaps the least controversial of taxes.'[51] Crosland overlooked what Hayek calls 'the natural instincts of parents to equip the new generation as well as they can'[52], and Tim Hames called 'the powerful psychological appeal to the idea that a little part of us carries on from beyond the grave through what we do with our financial bequest, particularly if it is handed to the children.'[53]

Indeed, the proposal by the Conservative Party to exempt large portions of accumulated wealth from inheritance tax (a move fiscal stringency will force to be postponed) proved so popular, even among the 94 per cent of people who are in no present danger of paying inheritance tax, that the Labour Government found itself forced to make a similar proposal lest it face an electoral disaster. The Government then had to find means of making up the resulting revenue deficiency, and decided to tax the very resource Smith warned should not bear a heavy burden – work and risk-taking, in this case by foreigners resident and working in the UK[54], and British entrepreneurs. Clearly, one among many examples of political expediency and a sense of what is fair, or at least politically expedient, trumping economists' notions of what is efficient.

Which is not a bad thing: arguments built on the notion that maximising economic efficiency is the sole goal of policy will not carry the day. Nor should they. Economists are most useful when they explain and, if possible, measure the costs and benefits of any policy proposal, and attempt to force politicians to confront those computations honestly. Democratically elected representatives might reasonably decide that the economic costs are worth bearing – that inheritance taxes, although more efficient than other revenue-raising measures, are abhorrently 'unnatural'; or that the health benefits of cleaner air are worth having even if the costs of scrubbing the air exceed the measured benefits.

This does not mean that economists should shut down their computers and confine themselves to the production of meaningless results from unrealistic models, leaving the policy world to others. Rather, they should accept, even if grudgingly, that their role in policy-making is not decisive. They serve as the polity's resource-bean-counters, the performers of the cost: benefits analyses to which politicians and society should pay heed. And, it is for the duly elected politicians to decide just who will be taxed, by how much, and, if I might

---

[51] Crosland, 1956, p.303.
[52] F.A. Hayek republished 2006, p. 80.
[53] Tim Hames, 'It's Time for the Last Rites Over Inheritance Tax', *The Times*, October 8, 2007.
[54] A mobile group that counts this author among its members.

borrow from Colbert, whose bed the feathers plucked from the tax-paying geese should feather.[55]

Here are a few suggestions designed to point them in a direction that balances the economist's desire for efficiency and the politician's desire for a tax system sufficiently fair – or at least seen as sufficiently fair – to enable him to continue in office.

Tax competition cannot be ignored, but it must be viewed in context. Low taxes in Darfur will not cause an exodus of hedge-fund managers from London or New York. It is the combination of the tax rate and the efficiency with which taxes are spent on transport, education, cultural amenities, and public safety that affects location decisions. The combination of high taxes and shoddy services is likely to prove lethal.

Complexity is as big a deterrent to potential investors as high taxes. Complexity creates compliance costs and the possibility of corruption by collectors who have wide discretion in determining just how much the taxpayer owes. If you doubt that, ask any Russian oligarch – if you can gain access to those now serving time for tax evasion. But keep in mind that most efforts to reduce complexity often increase it, and that investors can probably tolerate a suboptimal tax structure and rules better than changes in the structure and rules. Tinkering is a bad idea. Certainty matters.

So how high is high? The international norm for taxes on businesses seems to be settling around 25 per cent -30 per cent. 'When rates reach the 25-30 per cent range ... a country is in danger of pricing itself out of business. That is the range the UK finds itself in and has not helped by loading on excessive complexity, uncertainty, and unexpected changes in the tax code.'[56] But beware: the headline rate often bears little relation to the effective rate; credits for research and development, job creation and the like must be considered. Politicians often fail to dig beneath the headline rate to see what it is they are creating; businessmen and investors never fail to do so.

It is exceedingly important to make sensible estimates of the effect of proposed tax changes. There are taxes and there are taxes. Some have little effect on

---

[55] Jean Baptiste Colbert, finance minister to Louis XIV was renowned for the relentless manner in which he pursued sources of revenue for the Sun King. It is he who said, or didn't (the record is unclear), 'The art of taxation consists in so plucking the goose as to obtain the largest amount of feathers with the least amount of hissing.'

[56] John Cullinane, 'Tax Competition is More Complex Than Many Thought', *Financial Times*, March 27, 2008.

behaviour; others can produce changes that reduce the revenue anticipated from tax increases. Eschew both static analysis and the wildest claims of the supply-siders. This might be one place where well-constructed econometric models can prove useful.

Taxes should be concentrated on 'bads' not 'goods'. Pollution is a candidate for increased taxation; work and risk-taking should not be. And tax increases aimed at 'bads' such as pollution should be offset by lowering taxes on 'goods', rather than used as an excuse to increase the portion of private-sector wealth claimed by the state.

None of the above should reduce concern about the effect of taxes on the main well-spring of improved living standards – economic growth. The resources needed to grow any economy have become increasingly mobile, to varying degrees. That suggests that it is often wise to keep taxes on incomes low, lest the taxpayer flee, and concentrate on taxing consumption, with appropriate exemptions to reduce the regressive nature of some consumption taxes.

In the end, there is no simple solution to the problem created for policy-makers by the increased mobility of many of the factors of production and the seemingly ever-increasing demands of the welfare state. One part of any solution must be to keep costs manageable by increasing the productivity of the resources devoted to public service delivery, which means injecting competition and choice into the health care, education and other such industries. Another is to choose that combination of taxes that maximises economic growth, the ultimate source of rising living standards and a steady flow of revenues to the exchequer.

I know that it is a long way from these generalities to a tax code, which must be detailed. But if each detail is tested against these general propositions, the result might – just might – be tax levels and a tax structure that are both efficient and palatable.

Bibliography:

Barro, R.J., *Getting It Right: Markets and Choices in a Free Society*, Cambridge Mass., 1996.

Hayek, F.A., *The Constitution of Liberty*, London, 1960.

Coase, R.H., *Essays on Economics and Economists*, Chicago and London, 1994.

Elphicke, C., and W. Norton, *The Case For Reducing Business Taxes,* London, 2006.

Friedman, B.M., *The Moral Consequences of Economic Growth*, New York, 2005.

Himmelfarb, G., *The De-Moralization of Society: From Victorian Virtues to Modern Values*, London, 1995.

Lindsey, L.B., *The Growth Experiment: How The New Tax Policy Is Transforming the U.S. Economy*, New York, 1990.

Murray, C., *In Our Hands: A Plan to Replace the Welfare State*, Washington DC, 2006.

Office of National Statistics, *Labour Force Survey*, as reported by S.Hicks, *Trends in Public Sector* Employment, London, 2005.

Steuerle, E., 'Tax Policy From 1990 to 2001', in J. Frankel and P. Orszag (eds.) *American Economic Policy in the 1990s*, Cambridge Mass., 2002.

III
Tackling the Predatory State:
From High Tax Dirigisme to a New Liberalism

Deepak Lal

Introduction

Gordon Brown, when Chancellor of the Exchequer, set a trap on public spending and higher taxation: and all three political parties fell into it, showing no desire to challenge him on health and education spending. Even before the financial crisis the Conservatives had ruled out immediate tax cuts. All the political parties have embraced the *status quo* of a large, unreformed, welfare state with high levels of tax and spending. The position is like that of Butskellism. This post-war economic ideology dominated until questioned by Keith Joseph in the 1970s and repudiated by the Thatcher Governments in the 1980s. Since then the parties have been changing their clothes: Tony Blair stole the Conservatives' clothes and David Cameron is stealing New Labour's. All three parties seem prepared to spend over 40 per cent of our money on a range of activities including 'public services'. Neither opposition party questions whether health and education should in the main continue to be publicly provided and/or financed services, as at present; or indeed, why public funds are spent on a local and central government bureaucracy designed to address 'social exclusion'. The fiscal reforms which dramatically reduced public spending from 45 per cent of GDP in 1983 to 37.5 per cent in 1989 leaving it at 39.2 per cent when New Labour came to power have no current appeal in the party which pioneered them. The upshot is that there is now little to choose between the three parties when it comes to tax and spending.

The Tories, like their Swedish counterparts, appear to suggest they should be elected because the (overgrown) welfare state is safe in their hands; and they can run it more efficiently than their competitors. They have been intimidated by their 'progressive' opponents. They are mindful of the fact that nearly 50 per cent of the electorate has been made direct or indirect wards of the state. Any attack on the welfare state will, therefore, be opposed by a majority of dependants when they vote. As a result power will depend on accepting the new political reality and joining the 'progressive' social democratic tide.

Though the Swedish model is offered to prove that high levels of social security can be paid for from the cradle to the grave without damaging economic performance, the claim is false (see Figure 1). The Swedish economy, between 1870 and 1950, grew faster on average than any other industrialised economy, and the country became technologically one of the most advanced and richest in the world. From the 1950s Swedish economic growth slowed relative to other industrialised countries. This was due to the expansion of the welfare state and the growth of public – at the expense of private – employment.[57] After the Second World War the working population increased by about 1 million: public employment accounted for c. 770,000, private accounted for only 155,000. The crowding out by an inefficient public sector of the efficient private sector has characterised Sweden for nearly half a century.[58] From being the fourth richest county in the OECD in 1970 it has fallen to 14th place. Only in France and New Zealand has there been a larger fall in relative wealth. By contrast, Ireland, with economic reform and a low tax regime, improved its ranking from 21st place to 4th. Yet all the political parties in Britain now want to emulate the fabled Swedish model. David Hume and Adam Smith would not have been surprised.

This pamphlet will consider why this has happened. Why, on tax and spending, has political paralysis set in, other than a belated and vague acknowledgement that some cuts will have to be made? What has happened to the classical liberal principles and how has the collectivist impulse been channelled into a 'new dirigisme'? The new dirigisme must be countered by classical liberals as the first, essential, step towards the lower taxes and better public services the electorate as a whole wants.

Figure 1: GDP per capita, Sweden in relation to the average for sixteen industrialised countries 1870-1997. Constant prices. Index 1913=1

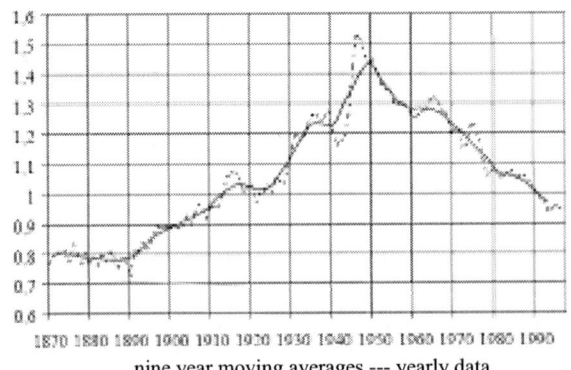

Source: O. Krantz, *Economic Growth and Economic Policy in Sweden in the 20th Century: A Comparative Perspective*, 2004

_____ nine year moving averages --- yearly data

[57] Krantz, 2004.
[58] Bacon and Eltis have shown this to be the central cause of the UK's economic decline in the 1960s and 1970s, though stalled and partially reversed by the Thatcher reforms of the 1980s. See Bacon and Eltis, 1976.

The predatory state: From monarch to middle classes

The power to tax is the 'power to take'. The State has this monopoly of coercion over its citizens. When absolute monarchs ruled, the interests of the people required that the 'power to take' should be restricted (as happened in the tax revolt which cost Charles I his head). Those who controlled the State were recognised, both in their origin and actions, to be self-interested predators. The monopoly of coercion provided the controllers of the State with the means to extract revenue from their prey. The State was in effect the equivalent of a Mafiosi protection racket. It is always inherently predatory and the interests of predators and their prey are not wholly divorced from each other. Predators to some extent are interested in the welfare of the prey which provides their own food supply. Similarly, self-interested predatory controllers of States have an interest in the welfare of their prey.

The prey needs the State for protection against external and internal aggression and to settle disputes between individuals. These ends – the classical public goods – prompt them to give the State the monopoly power of coercion and to finance itself from their earnings. But, once transferred to the sovereign, this power should not be used to extract more than necessary to finance public goods.

For the predatory State the 'power to take' allows it to extract from its prey when it can; or it allows a rival (external or internal) to provide the public goods at lower cost and contest its monopoly of coercion within the State. This is the dilemma of politics. How can the prey tie down an inherently predatory State to take only what is needed to provide the classical public goods?

When the State consisted of monarchs who took for themselves – for mistresses, palaces, armies and other paraphernalia of power – more than was needed to provide protection or other public goods, the dilemma was clear. At first the absolute monarch's 'power to take' was restricted by representative legislatures. But with the rise of majoritarian democracies, 'we' become the State if not the predator; and democratic governments also seek to maximise public revenue exercising discretionary power over its disposal.

Political parties, in two-party democratic systems, tend to serve the interest of the median voter, the 'power to take' having passed from absolute monarchs to the 'middle classes'. Why? Both parties in a two-party system will appeal to the interests of the median voter by occupying the middle ground. As much of democratic politics is redistributive, politicians serve the median voter by taking from those who are both richer and poorer through the welfare state tax-benefit systems of today's democracies. This is a form of transfer State. The US failure – by any party – to tackle middle class entitlements to social security, or the UK's to get the middle classes to pay for their children's higher education illustrate the phenomenon. Gordon Brown's success in making the 'median' voter a ward of the State has now been embraced by David Cameron who recognizes the reluctance of such voters to allow state hand-outs to be taken away.

Politicians do not just promote the interests of the median voter: they resemble the monopolistic revenue-maximising absolute monarchs of yore. Suppose, two parties announce their platforms successively.[59] The party to announce policy last can, by taxing some minority and transferring some of the revenue to a new majority, keep the rest for discretionary use and win. (One illustration of this is Gordon Brown's pledge to find savings from the current 'waste' in public services, to use it for his own purposes of 'investing' it – as he puts it – in public services).

Contemporary ethics do not, in most Western democracies, permit the direct transfer of the discretionary 'surplus' to politicians themselves. Instead it buys future votes, provides favours to 'friendly' interest groups, or – where close 'social' links exist between the politicians and bureaucrats – allows for an expanding bureaucracy. (One example is the former polytechnic lecturers who crowded the New Labour benches and social workers in local councils). There is then a continued interest in expanding the size of their 'bureaux' and budgets: to establish, maintain or expand monopoly of public provision of goods and services (including those which competitive private producers could provide more efficiently). Expanding the public sector leads to lucrative tenured jobs at the base of the bureaucratic pyramid and improves the future 'life chances' of bureaucrats in income, perquisites and power.

Though direct income transfers to government ministers are not now permitted in Western democracies, they are advocated for alleviating poverty. However, public servants do not favour direct non-discretionary monetary transfers to the 'poor', which give them little advantage. They prefer indirect and discretionary transfers which require the larger 'welfare bureaucracy', characteristic of the welfare state. With declining poverty in most industrial countries, new 'welfare' needs are discovered, for example that of 'social exclusion' (discussed below). This in turn leads to a further expansion of the

---

[59] This is not an essential assumption; the platforms could be announced simultaneously. See Brennan and Buchanan, 1980, pp. 20-23 for a fuller discussion. They also derive the set of taxes based on classical liberal principles which would limit predation by the State.

welfare bureaucracy.[60]

Just as the interventions of self-interested politicians and bureaucrats affect public finances, so too do the pressure groups into which individuals organize themselves. Election results will therefore reflect the interests of the most successful interest groups. Public policy will, as a result, be determined by competition among pressure groups, the most successful of which will be small and concentrated. As the income taken from the majority is spread over their members, the per capita costs to the 'losers' will be small and will rarely lead to the majority forming an opposing pressure group. Foreign trade protection advocated by producer interests, though contrary to consumer interests, can be explained in this way. One example is that of the protection offered to agricultural producers in the EU through CAP.

A further difficulty in checking the inherent predation of the State is the move from representative to participatory democracy. The increasing use of opinion polling in the political process in the United Kingdom and United States has led to this. With the median voters now seen as holding the key to electoral success, politicians need to know their opinions and interests to design the 'bribes' to be offered for votes; and they also need to train the spin doctors to win the rest of the electorate (through the altruistic rhetoric in which such self-seeking can be clothed).

The slide to participatory democracy is contrary to the Western notion of liberal democracy based on the representative principle. From the founding fathers of the American Republic to liberal thinkers like Immanuel Kant, direct or participatory democracy on the model of the Greek city-states has been held to be deeply illiberal. Subject to populist pressures and the changing passions of the majority, it can oppress minorities. By contrast, in a representative democracy, people choose their representatives for a legislature which legislates. The people do not themselves write or pass legislation. The representatives judge legislation on the merits of the case, moved ideally by reason. Edmund Burke's summary is as apt today as it was in 1774: 'Your representative owes you, not his industry only, but his judgment: and he betrays it instead of serving you if he sacrifices it to your opinion. You choose a member indeed; but when you choose him, he is not a member of Bristol, but he is a Member of Parliament'.[61]

---

[60] In any given week there are advertisements for the myriad of local authority jobs advertised weekly in *The Guardian*, so that one group or other of welfare workers can deal with perceived social exclusion.

[61] E. Burke, 1774 (1999).

The move towards direct participatory democracy has nonetheless taken place gradually in the US and UK. With the rise of the pollsters, and the weakening of party loyalties, politicians – particularly those of the 'third way' – have come to rely increasingly upon 'focus groups' to discover and pander to public opinion, the practice decried by Burke. By opening up the legislative process to greater scrutiny and accountability the system paradoxically becomes more open to influence by pressure groups and the phenomenon of *Demosclerosis*[62], where well-funded interest groups hijack domestic politics. Changes designed to democratise the system or to make it easier 'to listen to the people' have too often led to well-organized interest groups forcing governments to bend to their will. It is, as Zakaria put it, now clear that reforms 'designed to produce majority rule have produced minority rule',[63] as the people have neither the time nor the inclination to monitor the legislators' laws on a daily basis. As a result instead of rational consideration of alternative policies by the people's representatives, referenda determine the outcomes, often the consequence of 'spin' and emotion.

It might therefore seem quixotic to champion classical liberal principles for public finance. But even predatory political processes around the world have at various times yielded liberal reform.[64] The solution may lie in the theory of 'crisis and reform'.[65] A serious economic crisis, caused by the prey seeking through evasion, avoidance or flight to escape predation must occur so as to force the State to disgorge. Ideas help, but ultimately it is the interest of the State in overcoming the disorder its predation has bred that leads it to reverse direction.

Has the United Kingdom reached such a crisis in its social policies, with the NHS, schools and universities increasingly in disarray? Only time will tell. But when the crisis does arise and the median voter sees that with the prey fleeing, predation on this scale can no longer continue, the nature of reform must be clear. As numerous examples from around the world attest, the window of opportunity for reform is likely to be very small.

---

[62] Rauch, 1994.

[63] Zakaria, 2003.

[64] The Thatcher reforms which curbed the power of trade unions and dismantled the vast panoply of nationalised industries illustrate the point.

[65] This cycle of economic repression, crisis and reform was observed during the mercantilist period as documented in Eli Hecksher's magisterial book 'Mercantilism'. See D. Lal, 1987, pp.273-99. D. Lal and H. Myint, 1996.

State, economy and society: Rights and wrongs

The aim of political economy is to find how the State can provide the essential public goods at the least cost in terms of taxation. The classical liberals recognized the aim and laissez-faire economics provided a realistic approach where predatory governments were seen to put revenue maximisation above the social welfare maximisation of Platonic guardians. The classical policy prescriptions have been misrepresented.[66] The classical liberals were neither hostile to the State nor of the view that the role of governments in economic life was minor. Their view of the State was positive; and indeed[67] Adam Smith's view is almost identical to that of Keynes, who argued that 'the important thing for government is not to do things which individuals are doing already, but to do those things which at present are not done at all'.[68]

The State's three functions were recognised as (i) to protect society from foreign invaders, (ii) to protect each member from oppression and injustice by others and (iii) to provide and maintain the public works and institutions which provided public goods.[69] The principles of economic liberalism were set out in Mill's *Principles*, and their clearest modern reformulation is to be found in Hayek's *The Constitution of Liberty*. In fact, the current 'Washington Consensus' on economic policy is essentially a classical liberal policy package.[70]

---

[66] Caricatured by Carlisle's phrase 'anarchy plus the constable', or by Lasalles's simile of the night watchman

[67] Robbins, 1952.

[68] Keynes, 1926, pp 46-47.

[69] A. Smith, *The Theory of Moral Sentiments*, Indianapolis, 1982 (1759), .pp.184-5.

[70] The 'Washington Consensus' was the term coined by Williamson to describe the policy package which had emerged as best able to promote efficient poverty alleviating growth as a result of the experience of developing countries in the 1970s and 1980s. It is close to that advocated by A.C. Harberger, as constituting the best technocratic advice based on experience. It is also the one emerging from the Lal-Myint study of 25 developing countries. Recently Williamson has sought to disown it, partly because the anti-globalization backlash has used it, particularly in Latin America, as the whipping horse in its denouncement of what it calls the 'neo-liberal' policies adopted in Latin America. But, as Mario Vargas Llosa has argued, there are hardly any countries in Latin America, apart from Chile, who have in fact adopted the full package, and hence to announce its failure on the half-baked liberalization attempts in many countries is rather premature. T. N. Srinivasan rightly takes Williamson to task for his partial recantation.
J. Williamson, 'What Washington means by Policy Reform' in J. Williamson (ed.), 1990.
Harberger, 1984.
M. Vargas Llosa, 'Liberalism in the new millennium', in I.Vasquez (ed), 2000.
T. N. Srinivasan, *The Washington Consensus a decade later: ideology and the art and science of policy advice*, World Bank research Observer, vol.15, no.2, 2000, pp. 265-70

Classical liberals from Smith to Hayek to Friedman, have agreed that equality may be in conflict with liberty, and the liberal is not an egalitarian.[71] Classical liberals advocate public transfers, when private transfers are not available or sufficient to help the 'deserving poor'[72] and, since Mill, they have also advocated the public *financing* but not *provision* of merit goods such as health and education for those unable to afford them.[73] Though the programme promoted by social democrats increasingly resembles the classical liberal prescriptions, the exception is merit goods. In eschewing egalitarianism in taxation and by welfare state reform designed to concentrate the benefits to the 'deserving poor', both the New Democrats under Clinton in the United States and New Labour under Blair in the United Kingdom were closer to the classical liberal viewpoint than they imagine. The main difference is over the merit goods of health and education for which they believe that planned public provision should replace the operation of the market and that bureaucracy should be expanded to enforce various forms of political correctness. This is an enterprise view of the State as distinct from the State viewed as a civil association by classical liberals. These two views of the State – that of civil association with no purposes of its own and that of an enterprise seeking to legislate some vision of perfectibility – have been the two dominant voices in Western political thought and action: one going back to the Greeks, the other being part of the Judaeo-Christian tradition.

The New Dirigisme: The rise of the 'enterprise' voice of socialism towards the end of the 19th century led to 'the end of laissez-faire'.[74] The erosion of the classical liberal 'civil association' view of the State had begun in Europe with Bismarck's social insurance scheme in Germany and the liberal welfare reforms in Britain of 1906-14. It spread to the United States during the Great Depression and Roosevelt's New Deal. The dominant ideology which was to follow – 'embedded liberalism' or 'social democracy'[75] – was encouraged by the economists; and by the Second World War the 19th century classical liberalism had been replaced by the dirigiste dogma, especially pronounced in the Communist countries. With their demise after the Berlin Wall fell, the socialist impulse has been transformed. Rather than seeking to replace capitalism, it wishes to create 'capitalism with a human face'. Moreover, the

---

[71] Hayek, 1960, p.402.

[72] See the discussion in Lal and Myint, *The Political Economy of Poverty, Equity and Growth*, 1996.

[73] In D. Lal, *Nationalised Universities - paradox of the privatisation age*, London, 1989, I have outlined how this can be done for higher education in the UK and in D. Lal, *A Premium on health: A National Health Insurance Scheme*, London, 2001, how the NHS can be reformed in line with these principles.

[74] Keynes, 1926

[75] Eichengreen, 1996.

notion of freedom has been used to promote the 'enterprise' views of the State under cover of an implied view of the State as a 'civil' association by using the distinction between negative and positive freedom, and by arguing that the promotion of 'positive freedoms' is no different from the promotion of negative freedom, which classical liberals value.[76]

'Freedom' and 'liberty': The economist-philosopher Anthony de Jasy has provided classical liberals with an escape from this dirigiste trap. Jasay jettisons the notion of freedom as being central to classical liberalism. The most basic reason for not relying on the concept of freedom to justify a classical liberal society and polity is that freedom in ordinary speech involves ensuring that deliberate obstacles are not being placed in the way of individuals' actions. This immediately leads to the slippery slope, where 'being *free* to do something and being *able* to do it' are elided. The discourse of freedom then degenerates into one in which freedom means the general availability to all of the good things of life. This allows various policies forming part of the socialist enterprise view of the world to be smuggled in as being part of freedom.[77]

Instead Jasay, relying on the English common law tradition, defines the rules which the State as a civil association should uphold. These are Mill's principles of liberty: a person can undertake any *feasible* action which does not harm others or break an obligation.[78] The burden of proof lies on someone who wants to prohibit an individual's actions. This process is equivalent to the presumed innocence of the accused unless found guilty by due process. In contrast to this common law tradition of justice there is an alternative which may be called the continental system of justice, or 'public law' as Jasay calls it. Under this, individuals are forbidden from feasible actions unless they are expressly *permitted* by various 'rights' granted under constitutional provisions.

Of the two alternative legal traditions, the common law based on a list of *prohibited* actions, is more readily verifiable than the public law tradition based on a list of *permitted* actions. For feasible actions are limitless, and listing what we must not do is less onerous than listing what we are permitted to do.[79] If

---

[76] As discussed by I. Berlin, *Two concepts of Liberty*, in his Four Essays on Liberty, Oxford, 1969.
[77] See Sen, 1999, Sugden, 1993.
[78] De Jasay, 1996, .p.23.
[79] If, as is usually the case, there is no clear boundary to the possible harms a particular action could cause, it will be impossible to prove that a feasible action is harmless. Similarly with obligations (which confer corresponding rights), it will be impossible to prove that some right has not been violated. In the common law tradition the *prosecutor* has to prove that, in pursuing a particular action, the defendant has violated obligations or caused harm to others. In the continental law tradition it is for the *defendant* to prove that he has not violated *any* right or caused *any* possible harm.

the 'liberty' norm of the common law tradition based on prohibitions of feasible actions is more sound (being verifiable) than the continental tradition based on permissions, what of 'property rights' and 'human rights'?[80]

Property rights: Property rights are mistakenly called rights. If an individual is free to do something which is not wrong, this liberty must include the freedom to do what he likes with his property. *Liberties are different from rights*. While the property owner has the *liberty* to use his property, the non-owner has to get the *right* to use it which is provided by the lease. Thus, whereas liberties are not conferred by anyone, rights require someone else to have agreed to fulfill some obligation.

Ownership is often acquired through the proceeds of work, through exchange (e.g. like that of assets) or from gifts and inheritance. These means of acquiring property meet the requirements of justice; they involve exercising a liberty without transgressing any obligation or causing harm to others.

Conquest and seizure have been equally important in acquiring land. The means are morally unjust and calls for restitution would be justified. This is at the heart of the controversy about the Palestinians' 'right to return' in the Arab-Israeli dispute. But, though the claim may be morally just, it is not expedient. For most societies throughout history have recognised the chaos that would be caused by seeking to redress every fault in the historical descent of every current title to property, no matter how far back the chain of transfers stretches. They have, therefore, (correctly) applied some form of statute of limitations – if for no other reason than recognising that the sins of the fathers should not be visited upon their grandchildren and great-grandchildren.

Human rights: What of 'human rights?' Rights (as already mentioned) arise from contracts – actual or implicit – which give rise to obligations that have been accepted by someone else. Thus 'every right of one person has the *agreement* of another as its source, cause and evidence'.[81] Agreement is crucial in generating rights and the corresponding obligations. Thus social rights are not rights but *entitlements*. The right of the unemployed to unemployment insurance or the poor to welfare are not rights, but entitlements created by the

---

[80] Nozick, 1974, p.92. Jasay's position on rights is different from R. Nozick. One of the senses in which Nozick uses rights: 'rights that is permissions to do something and obligations on others not to interfere' Jasay rightly notes 'rights are not permissions but claims for performance by another. Yet liberties are not permissions either; if they were they would be most confusingly misnamed. Who would be competent to grant permissions and on what authority?'. He also contests Nozick's position on property rights, see his, n.2, p.5-51.
[81] De Jasay, 1996, p.30.

State, which can be changed or repudiated because they are not based on contract. By contrast a genuine right arising from a contract cannot be limited or withdrawn without the right holder giving his consent. These rights are sometimes called *specific* rights.

In addition the claim is made for 'human rights' - a *general* right – which arise from the assumption that being *human* justifies certain rights which go beyond specific rights. They are the descendants of 'natural rights'.[82] They arise from the general right, namely 'the equal right of all men to be free'[83], including the right to free speech, free worship, to walk about, to breathe. However such a 'right' is redundant in the Common Law tradition where one is free to act provided it does not infringe one's obligations (the specific rights of others) or cause others harm.[84] Only in the Public Law tradition do these 'rights' need to be specified where all feasible actions require *permission,* including these 'human rights' to breathe, to be able to speak freely, to walk around etc.[85] Individual freedom of action is much better protected by the common law tradition where one is free to take any feasible action subject to the constraints of harm and specific obligations (rights).

Capitalism with a human face: Many of capitalism's opponents use the concept of freedom to imply an 'enterprise' view of the state, yet appear also to subscribe to the classical liberal view of the State as a 'civil' association. They aim to justify redistributive measures. Their position is one of denying that distribution of property based on contract, transfers, and first possession can be just. Instead they view property as arising from the mutual gains provided by social co-operation.

The claim is that much existing wealth is the result of social co-operation going back to Adam and Eve. It is a social inheritance and belongs to the whole of society. But, largely for reasons of efficiency, it is inexpedient to rule out some private appropriation of this social wealth. Hence, some social wealth can be converted into private property, on the terms and conditions specified by the co-owner society.

---

[82] Minogue, 1979

[83] Hart, 1967

[84] Isaiah Berlin refers to human rights as 'a frontier of freedom' which no one is allowed to cross (p.165). But as Little rightly notes: 'an infinite list of rights is not convincing as a frontier. The frontier is properly constituted by the quite limited list of things that one may not do to human beings'.

[85] But as there are infinite number of such 'rights', it will be impossible to delineate them all, which would give rise to endless legalistic disputes.

This can be done provided social exclusion from this social wealth – of those disadvantaged by lack of talent, luck or who are unable to share in the benefits of social co-operation – is prevented. The State as the co-owner of this social wealth should use its powers to coerce some to give up part of their property or income to the disadvantaged.

The false premise is that individual contributions to past and present social co-operation and wealth are impossible to trace and all wealth is seen as that generated by society as a whole.

But, though social co-operation has generated the wealth in the world, it is false to claim that no trace of the individual contributions is available. Everyone who has contributed through work has been paid in voluntary exchanges. Some payments were consumed, some saved and invested and the resulting assets have the contributors' title to them. To coerce them to give away what is theirs – and which they are at liberty to use as they see fit would – be unjust. Though over the millennia everyone has contributed to the generation and accumulation of a society's wealth, this does not mean that everything is owed to society. *'Nothing is owed'* Jasay rightly notes, 'everything has been paid for, one way or another, in a manner and to an extent sufficient to call forth the contribution. There is no further common-pool claim overhanging the lot, for no payment must be made twice. He who sees an overhanging claim in favour of 'society' is seeing a mirage, or the wishful image of one'.[86]

In the same way it is false to claim that because social co-operation is needed for gains in a business or corporation, everyone is a *stakeholder*, to be consulted and if necessary assuaged. A corporation consists of a series of voluntary exchanges based on a contract where the worker is obliged to perform certain tasks in payment for the agreed remuneration. The obligation to consult may be given by the employer to the worker, as part of the contract and in this way a specific right is granted matching the voluntarily agreed obligation.[87] But

---

[86] De Jasay, 1996, p.51.

[87] Coase, 1937. The existence of corporations depends upon there being various contracts which cannot be specified at arm's length. Because workers acquire various skills which are specific to the firm through on the job training, this form of firm-specific capital is of value to the firm but not the the worker who cannot cash them my moving to another firm. These firm specific skills are to be distinguished from the general skills acquired from on the job training which can be marketed outside the firm. Because of the importance of firm level skills there will have to be a more permanent relationship between employer and employee than the arm's length transactions of a spot market for labour. This means that the employer will now have to incur the policing type of transactions costs in monitoring workers to see that they are not shirking. This would require the hierarchical organization of firms. As part of this task the

there can be no general right to consult 'stake- holders', unless one believes that the sharing of the fruits of co-operation cannot be assigned by voluntary contract, and hence this social product has to be shared by continual negotiation or mediation by the co-owner of society's capital – the State. For the dirigistes the employer's capital has been leased to him from society's capital owned by the State on its behalf. The claim is false. The employer has justly acquired capital from past savings and can do with them what he pleases. There is nothing which belongs to society which has been leased out to the employer.

Another illegitimate claim is that the economic power wielded by employers and corporations is coercive and forces the weak to give into the demands of the strong. That confuses the *actual options* open to the weaker party (where they can act freely on the offer of the employer) with their *hopes* for a better deal.[88] However, it would be unjust to use the coercive power of the state to enforce this hope of the weak and violate the stronger party's liberty to use their endowments as they wish.

In the same way other State coercion to take a person's justly acquired property to give it to anyone else would also be ruled out where the State is seen as a civil association. Inheritance taxes would be ruled out; other redistributive taxes would be unjust. Would public transfers to the destitute be ruled out? Most societies have made provision for the destitute: those incapable of making any living. The safety net has usually been provided through private transfers from other family members or public charity. With the fraying of families in the West these private social safety nets have also become frayed. Public charity remains the only alternative. Therefore where private charity can no longer be relied on to alleviate destitution, some form of public transfers may be forthcoming.[89]

What kind of tax for the global economy?

How then can the fiscal exactions of democratic, predatory states be

---

employer may choose various forms of contracts with the workers which could include 'co-determination' like having workers on boards of companies. But given the diversity of conditions faced by different firms, in a free market, the types of contracts will be varied, including the types advocated by promoters of 'stakeholder capitalism'. What would go against the functioning of the free market was if a particular type of contract, viz. the stakeholder type, was forced on all employers by legislative fiat.

[88] This can be seen as part of the set of feasible actions they can take, based on the offer made by the strong, which does not infringe the rules of justice that the owner is free to dispose of his endowment as long as he does not violate the constraints of harm and obligation.

[89] Lal and Myint, 1996

controlled? How can the fiscal privileges inherent in the government's power to take and give to whom it chooses be limited? Two different answers are given, both from Nobel Prize winners. The first is that of the 'optimum tax theory', for which James Mirlees won the Nobel Prize, but which goes back to the Cambridge mathematician Frank Ramsey in the 1920s. The idea is that the optimum pattern of taxation to raise a given revenue is higher taxes levied on goods for which the price elasticity of demand (which measures the sensitivity of the quantity of the good consumed to its price) is low (e.g. cigarettes and alcohol). It assumes (falsely) a benevolent government.[90]

But, suppose if instead of a benevolent government seeking to raise a *given* revenue we have a predatory government which wants to raise the *maximum* revenue it can, what set of taxes will it choose? These are Ramsey's optimal taxes which a consumer (e.g. an addicted smoker facing a tax on cigarettes) finds inescapable.[91]

The only taxes which citizens should grant to a predatory state, says the other Nobel Prize winner, James Buchanan and others, are those from which people can escape – those for goods with elastic demand. In the same way for providing local public goods there should be local sales taxes in a decentralized fiscal system, with tax competition between localities limiting their predation, not taxes on property or wealth. All sides agree, however, that the base of the tax system, should, ideally be consumption and not income.

Recent proposals for flat taxes to limit the fiscal predation of governments should be considered in this context. A flat tax, in its pure version, replaces

---

[90] These set of optimum taxes were derived by Frank Ramsey, a Cambridge mathematician, as the formal answer to a puzzle set him in the 1920's by A. C. Pigou. What set of taxes would minimize loss of welfare to raise a *given* revenue? Ramsey's answer was that the optimum pattern of taxation was to impose higher taxes on goods for which (in economists' jargon) the price elasticity of demand was low – like cigarettes and alcohol. Imposing such taxes would reduce the excess burden (in terms of loss of consumers surplus) associated with raising a given revenue. The explanation: suppose that there are two goods: cigarettes, for which price elasticity is low, so that when their price rises, consumption does not drop substantially; and restaurant meals, for which the price elasticity is high, so that an equivalent percentage increase in their price reduces their consumption substantially. As a welfare measure of the loss of satisfaction to consumers depends on the reduction in of the quantity of good consumed induced by the price rise, the tax on cigarettes will involve a lower loss of consumer satisfaction than a tax yielding equivalent revenue on restaurant meals.

[91] It is Ramsey's optimal tax, because the tax yield from any given ad valorem tax on cigarettes in inelastic demand will be greater than an equivalent tax on restaurant meals with an elastic demand. Because of their addiction smokers will find the tax on cigarettes inescapable, whilst consumers of restaurant meals being more easily able to reduce their consumption can escape the tax.

multiple marginal rates with a single marginal rate; it also abolishes the complex systems of allowances and reliefs used by governments to buy votes or for social engineering. A high personal tax-free allowance allows the poor to be taken out of the tax net and imparts progressivity to the system. All taxes – corporate, personal income, and commodity taxes (e.g. VAT) – are set at the same rate, amounting in effect to a consumption tax which abolishes any double taxation (such as that of dividends). The flat tax has the advantage of simplicity and transparency (which lead to greater tax compliance and increased tax revenues), faster economic growth (due to greater incentives to work) and the removal of disincentives and distortions in existing tax systems. The main costs in the short run could be a loss of revenue with the reduction in rates and the increased income tax threshold to help low earners. The UK treasury in its uncensored version of the flat tax found support for many of these beneficial effects to the UK economy from a flat tax.[92]

The major advantage from a classical liberal viewpoint is that the flat tax prevents governments from politically inspired redistribution. But whereas the East European countries which adopted the flat tax were replacing defunct tax regimes, in developed countries mature tax systems are based on such a redistribution game over many generations. The likely losers would be the middle classes, the former beneficiaries who would resist the flat tax. So, even though a number of developed countries, including the U.K., Germany, Spain Greece and Italy are considering a flat tax, it is unlikely to be of the pure form. According to George Osborne, the Shadow Chancellor and a British supporter, that also would probably be the case in the UK. If, however, a flat-tax could be implemented, it would, on account of its transparency and simplicity, make it more difficult for governments to increase predatory public expenditure. *All* taxpayers would know it implied a rise in the flat tax they would have to pay. This should aid the tax resistance of all the prey who can no longer be played off one against another by the predatory state.

The signs are that developed countries like the UK may adopt the classical liberal principles on tax and spending on account of the growing tax competition from the new economies of Asia and Eastern Europe. Many of the emerging economies are, because of their own economic reforms, low tax and spend economies. Based on classical liberal principles China has undertaken the largest unilateral trade liberalization since the UK's repeal of the Corn Laws in the 19th century. If they can resist the siren pressures for the European 'social model', they will increasingly provide a more congenial environment for footloose capital from around the world. As their per capita incomes rise

---

[92] See http://www.hm-treasury.gov.uk./media/CFA/92/foi_flattax010805.pdf

and they attract home their 'best and the brightest', the United States and United Kingdom will find it increasingly difficult to use the present 'brain drain' from Asia to reverse the damage done to their indigenous human capital formation by failed public education systems. Perhaps this will lead to the crisis of the welfare state which alone will persuade the median voter in these countries to abandon continuing *dirigisme* and adopt the classical liberal principles they still, at least, rhetorically espouse.

The catalyst for change: competition

As the global economic picture changes new and successful economies are poised to challenge the survival of older high tax and spending countries. Western politicians must therefore grapple anew with one of the oldest economic problems: How can lower taxes and better public services become the natural order. How can the State, by nature predatory and with monopoly power of coercion, be forced only to extract what is needed for the basic classical public goods - defence, law and order – financing merit goods (for those unable to afford them) and alleviating destitution? Today the problem has come full circle, as the concept of 'freedom' which provided a basis for controlling the predator, is used to justify the predatory state.

Whereas the classical liberals recommended laissez faire as the best way of tying down the state, their socialist successors promoted the dogma of state enterprise, central control and dirigisme. Even after socialism's demise, the dirigisme – the way in which the State fulfils its inherently predatory instincts – was not reversed. Rather the socialist impulse found a new voice advocating a 'new dirigisme'. It appropriated the (classical liberal) ideal of freedom and championed predatory dirigiste policies in the name of 'positive' freedom. New Labour's legacy is a burgeoning nanny state based on moral and social paternalism, and an intricate web of stealth taxes which` has considerably raised the State's 'take' to finance unreformed public services. The upshot is that in the UK today, Government and Opposition parties all seem to want to imitate Sweden's tax and spend policies. But just as Sweden has slipped in the growth league because of its over extended welfare state, the UK's previous economic boom – largely due to the Thatcher reforms – has been dramatically stifled by this new dirigisme.

What then does the future hold? How can the UK ensure economic prosperity with a fiercely competitive global market? At a theoretical level, the new dirigisme (in the name of 'positive freedom') can be curbed by distinguishing 'freedom' from 'liberty' as enshrined in the Common Law tradition. If economic as well as social policy is once again based on classical liberal principles it will serve the interests of the prey who want lower taxes and better public services. In particular the UK must address two developments.

First, the growing economic competition from the emerging economies of Asia and Europe with its potentially serious implications for the UK's economic future, must be understood and met. These new and successful economies have relatively low spending and tax, where the UK's by contrast is high. As a result these new economies may attract both footloose capital and (given time) their bright and able nationals who currently work abroad. That would lead to the flight of much needed capital for investment from the UK and it would reverse the brain drain, now seen as helping to sustain an increasingly unsustainable dirigiste economy in the United Kingdom. So the United Kingdom must change course if it is to maintain its prosperity.

Second the ever increasing appetite by the state for funds to feed un-reformable public health and educational systems could lead to a crisis. Just as in the 1970s nationalized industries eventually compelled reform, so now these nationalized public services may do likewise. When that happens, the – classical liberal – principles which have already shaped reform, that of tax and spending and that of moribund industries, may once again provide the solution to the crisis. The state must then denationalize and allow the winds of competition and freedom to blow.

Bibliography:

Bacon, R. & W. Etlis, *Britain's Economic Problem: Too Few Producers*, London, 1976.

Berlin, I., 'Two concepts of Liberty', in his *Four Essays on Liberty*, Oxford, 1969.

Brennan, G. & J. Buchanan, *The Power To Tax* , Cambridge, 1980.

Burke, E. 'Speech to the Electors of Bristol' in Payne, J., *Selected Workes of Edmund Burke* vol.iv, Indianapolis, 1774 (1999).

Coase, R.H., 'The Nature of the Firm' *Economica*, n.s.4, 1937.

De Jasay, A., *Before Resorting to Politics*, Aldershot, 1996.

Eichengreen, B., *Globalizing Capital*, Princeton NJ, 1996.

Harberger, A.C., *World Economic Growth*, San Francisco, 1984.

Hart, H., 'Are there any Natural Rights?' in A. Quitnon (ed) *Political Philosophy*, Oxford, 1967.

Hayek, F., *The Constitution of Liberty*, Chicago, 1960.

Keynes J.M., *The End of Laissez-Faire*, London, 1926.

Krantz, O., *Economic growth and Economic Policy in Sweden in the 2oth Century: A Comparative Perspective*, Ratio Work Paper No.32, London, 2004.

Lal, D., *The Political Economy of Economic Liberalisation*, World Bank Economic Review vol.1 no.2, 1987.

Lal, D., *Nationalised Universities - paradox of the privatisation age*, London, 1989.

Lal, D. & H. Myint, *The Political Economy of Poverty, Equity and Growth – a comparative study*, Oxford, 1996.

Lal, D., *A Premium on health: A National Health Insurance Scheme*, London, 2001.

Llosa, M.V., 'Liberalism in the New Millennium' in I. Vasquez (ed.) *Global Fortune*, Washington DC, 2000.

Minogue, K., 'The history of the idea of Human Rights', in W. Laquer and R. Rubin (eds): *The Human Rights Reader*, New York, 1979.

Nozick, R., *Anarchy, State and Utopia*, Oxford, 1974.

Rauch, J., *Demosclerosis: The Silent Killer of American Government*, New York, 2004.

Robbins, L., *The Theory of Economic Policy in English Classical Political Economy*, London, 1952.

Sen, A.K., *Development as Freedom*, Oxford, 1999.

Smith, A., *The Theory of Moral Sentiments*, Indianapolis, 1759 (1982).

Srinavasan, T.N., 'The Washington Consensus a decade later: ideology and the art and science of policy advice', *World Bank Research Observer*, vol.15, no.2, 2000

Sugden, R., 'A review of 'Inequality reexamined' by A. Sen, *Journal of Economic Literature*, vol.31, no.4, 1993.

Williamson, J., 'What Washington Means by Policy Reform' in J. Williamson (ed), *Latin American Adjustment: How Much Has Happened?*, Washington DC, 1990.

Zakaria, F., *The Future of Freedom*, New York, 2003.

IV
Tax and Benefits for the Future
Social Accounts in an Efficient, Fair Tax Transfer System

Peter Birch Sørensen and Arij Lans Bovenberg

Introduction: The Need for Reform

Today, redistribution from the rich to the poor is seen as a basic function of the modern welfare state. This redistribution operates through tax and social insurance systems, such as the UK national insurance system. Voters, however, tend to disagree on how far governments should pursue tax and benefit goals. This is largely because of the tough trade-offs which characterise redistribution of income and social insurance. The trade-offs - between equity and economic efficiency and between insurance and incentives – are, by their nature, controversial. Governments may achieve a more equal distribution of income by levying taxes and offering transfers, but taxes and transfers weaken the incentives to work, save and invest, reducing the size of the 'pie' available for redistribution. Moreover, by insuring against income risks through social transfers, governments blunt the individual incentives of the people themselves to prevent, where possible, the various contingencies (like unemployment or sickness). This phenomenon known as 'moral hazard' also reduces total output and income.

In recent years globalisation, population ageing and technological change have tended to worsen these trade-offs. Globalisation increases the international mobility of capital and labour, hampering the ability of governments to impose redistributive taxes and to offer social benefits without inducing the rich to emigrate (or to export their wealth) and without attracting poor immigrants. Moreover, the rising ratio of retirees to people of working age increases the tax cost of providing a given level of public pensions, health care and other services to the elderly. At the same time rapid technological change, biased against low-skilled workers, increases the unemployment risks that the low-skilled face, and raises therefore the cost of offering effective unemployment insurance.

The changing nature of such social risks also puts the welfare state under pressure. As the economy shifts from blue-collar work in industrial sectors to white-collar work in service sectors and knowledge-intensive activities, mental causes of sickness and disability become more prominent. These types of sickness and disability are harder to diagnose than those with physical causes; as a result it is more difficult to verify whether a potential recipient is in fact eligible for a social insurance benefit. Changes in technology and the organisation of work have also made many segments of the labour market more 'fluid', as people move more often between jobs and in and out of the labour market. In such a transitional labour market it is more difficult to establish whether a person is voluntarily or involuntarily out of work; the problem of moral hazard in unemployment insurance is exacerbated.

These developments increase the costs both of income redistribution and social insurance. At the same time the dynamic world economy, with its rapid technological progress and changing patterns of international trade, leads to greater risks for people and greater need of social insurance.

As a result the trade-offs between equity and efficiency and between insurance and incentives have deteriorated in recent years. Against this background governments are looking for ways to redesign their tax-transfer systems so that the goals of redistribution and social insurance are secured at a lower cost in terms of economic efficiency.

This chapter offers a blueprint for reforming social insurance systems (including the UK's national insurance system). It will argue that partial financing through mandatory individual savings accounts could make a large number of taxpayers better off without making anybody worse off, provided such a system is combined with a guaranteed minimum level of social protection for the lifetime poor.

The reform proposal focuses on the financing of social transfers to citizens of working age. Though it does not need simultaneous reform of old-age pensions, the individual accounts for the working population could be integrated with the pension system and the third section will show how.

To help the reader evaluate the reform proposal, the next section will address the basic functions of social insurance, clarify some alternative concepts of redistribution, and present empirical estimates of the degree to which the social insurance systems in some modern welfare states succeed in redistributing lifetime incomes from the rich to the poor. The proposal for social insurance reform will then be considered in detail and an illustration given of how it might work in practice and the implications, using the Danish welfare state as a case study. The data will suggest parallels between the UK and Danish systems. The discussion will conclude with an assessment of the proposed reform from a broader economic, social and political perspective and its advantages for a government focussed on fiscal reform in a modern welfare state which promotes incentive.

How Do Welfare States Redistribute?

Social Insurance: Aims and Objects

Social insurance for the working population aims to protect citizens against large income losses caused by unemployment, sickness, disability and other social events that temporarily or permanently reduce or eliminate their capacity to earn income. Britain's national insurance system was initially envisaged as a form of social insurance system and is supposed to serve the same function of protection against lost income. In theory people whose income fluctuates could protect themselves against these income risks and smooth their consumption over time through different means: by undertaking precautionary saving for rainy days, by borrowing when their income was temporarily low, or by taking out private insurance against various contingencies. However, problems of imperfect and asymmetric information that prevent a perfect functioning of private markets for credit and insurance mean that such a laissez-faire solution would leave many citizens with little protection. For example, a potential lender may not know enough about the future earnings capacity of an unemployed person to be willing to offer him credit against his expected future income. Similarly, when insurance companies do not have the information needed to distinguish (fully) the 'good risks' from the 'bad risks' among their customers, they cannot differentiate (fully) insurance premiums according to risk. Hence they will tend to overcharge the good risks and undercharge the bad ones, thus deterring the former customers and attracting only the latter ones, possibly to the point where it becomes unprofitable to offer any insurance at all.

Even though the government is also imperfectly informed, it can use its taxing power to pool the risks among all taxpayers; it can make sure that the money that it pays out to people in need is balanced in the aggregate through tax receipts. Through the tax-transfer system the government can force the good as well as the bad risks to participate in a system of social insurance in those cases where the opting-out behaviour of the good risks cause private insurance markets to fail.

One of the basic functions of social insurance is to offer *liquidity insurance* enabling people who could not otherwise obtain (sufficient) credit or insurance to maintain an acceptable living standard in periods of temporary income losses. Of course, the government, rather than pay out a social insurance benefit without obliging the beneficiary to repay later, could lend the amount to the citizen in temporary need and oblige him to repay the money with interest and with instalments conditional on his future earnings. An example in the sphere of education is the UK's student loan system. However, governments tend to choose the former because social insurance serves another objective, that of *equity*: it allows income to be redistributed from those with good luck to those with bad luck.

Discussions of redistributive policies usually take a short-term perspective, focusing on redistribution of annual incomes or at least incomes earned over a relatively short time. However, a person's annual income is often a very poor indicator of his lifetime earnings capacity, since individual earnings tend to vary a lot over the life cycle. An obvious example is a student in higher education who may have a very low income while being educated but who may end up with a high lifetime income as a result of the extra earnings capacity generated by his education. Similarly, a parent withdrawing temporarily from the labour market to care for a small child may earn nothing during that period but may still earn a respectable income over the long run after having re-entered the labour market. Another example is a person suffering a single spell of, say, six months of unemployment during his entire working career. During that particular year he may be pushed to the bottom of the income distribution even if he ends up in a much higher bracket of the distribution of lifetime incomes.

This suggests that *as long as the system of social insurance provides adequate liquidity insurance against temporary income losses*, the objective of redistribution should be specified in terms of *lifetime* rather than *annual* incomes, since a person's lifetime income is a much better indicator of his long-term earnings capacity than his annual income. In other words, apart from offering liquidity insurance, the other basic function of the system of social insurance is to *redistribute lifetime income* from those with good luck to those with bad luck in life. A person's lifetime income may be low if earnings capacity is harmed over a large part of his working career: this can be due to circumstances beyond his control – e.g. a number of spells of cyclical unemployment. Lifetime income may also be low if he is unlucky to be born with limited innate abilities; or the development of his potential for learning or the social skills needed to succeed in the labour market may be hampered if the individual grows up in a disadvantaged background. Most people would agree that it is fair to redistribute income in favour of disadvantaged citizens: and this is most effectively done if redistributive policies focus on the distribution of lifetime rather than annual incomes.

It can be argued that all citizens, at least up to a point, benefit from a tax-transfer system that redistributes lifetime income; such a system can be seen as an insurance device from the perspective of (the parents of) unborn and young children who do not know their future position in society. If they end up with bad luck in life, the social insurance system will protect them; if they are risk averse, they will be willing to pay a price for this protection in the form of the taxes they must pay if they end up being well off.

Of course, a person's realised lifetime income is not a perfect indicator of his capacity to earn income. For example, a person with a good earnings capacity may still end up with a relatively low lifetime income if for some reason he chooses not to work very hard or if he impairs his earnings potential through irresponsible behaviour. Ideally one would like to redistribute in favour of individuals with low earnings *capacities* rather than low *actual* earnings, at least to the extent that low realised earnings are the outcome of a deliberate individual choice which can be reversed. However, in practice policy-makers can only observe the actual incomes of individuals (and even that is sometimes very difficult!), so a person's realised lifetime income remains the best available indicator of his earnings capacity.

In summary, the basic goals of social insurance are to provide liquidity insurance against temporary income losses and to redistribute lifetime incomes. The reform proposed below will be judged against these criteria.

How to Redistribute: From Rich to Poor or over the Life Cycle?
Existing public transfer programmes tend to be focused on the redistribution of annual rather than lifetime incomes. As a consequence, much of the redistribution achieved by modern welfare states is a *redistribution over the individual's life cycle* - also known as *intra*-personal redistribution - rather than so-called *inter*-personal redistribution from the lifetime rich to the lifetime poor. In other words, a large fraction of the taxes currently levied to finance social insurance benefits is essentially money that the taxpayer transfers to himself over the life cycle rather than a transfer of lifetime incomes across different individuals. Over the course of his life a person pays taxes, and a part of those taxes finances the various benefits he receives at various points in his career, e.g. benefits received during spells of unemployment and sickness, education grants, child and family benefits, etc. However, since there is rarely a direct link between taxes paid and benefits received, the taxes and benefits tend to distort economic behaviour, mostly by discouraging work and encouraging the take-up of benefits even if they are not really needed.

The recent evidence from a sample of Western countries including the UK, Denmark, Italy and Sweden shows that a large part of the tax bill tends to be redistributed, not from rich to poor but to the taxpayer over his lifetime. The figures for the UK are between 62 per cent and 71 per cent for intra-personal redistribution and between 29 per cent and 38 per cent for inter-personal redistribution. For Denmark, Italy and Sweden the figures are of the same order (Table 2). A more detailed examination of the Danish figures will be helpful in illustrating the position.

The Danish social insurance system provides a striking example of the degree of 'churning' in modern Western European welfare states, that is, the higher proportion of intra-personal relative to inter-personal redistribution. Table 1 summarises the most recent estimates of the impact of the Danish tax-transfer system on the distribution of lifetime incomes. The estimates were produced by the Danish Economic Council, based on a comprehensive data set covering a representative 10 per cent sample of the Danish population above 18.[93] The table groups the population into ten deciles according to the size of their total accumulated lifetime income before taxes and transfers ('market income'). Thus the column headed D1 shows average figures for the poorest 10 per cent of the population; the column headed D2 gives average figures for the second-poorest 10 per cent of the population, etc., so the column D10 indicates the average numbers for the richest 10 per cent of all individuals.

The first row in Table 1 shows the average lifetime market incomes in the different income groups. The second row, 'Taxes reserved for social insurance', shows estimates of that part of the direct and indirect tax bill which serves to finance the various social insurance programmes, while the third column indicates the total social insurance benefits received by individuals in each income group over their life cycles. Individuals receiving social transfers in a given year also pay some amount of tax (at least indirect tax) during that same year. If taxes paid during the year exceed the benefits received, the benefits can be said to be fully financed by the taxpayer himself, and if the tax bill amounts to, say, half the benefits collected during the year, the taxpayer has self-financed half of his benefit income in the same year. The fourth column in Table 1 shows the amount of direct and indirect taxes that the various income groups paid in return for benefits received during the same year of their life. Another part of the transfers received over the life cycle is financed by the recipient himself via the taxes paid in the other years of life. This self-financing of benefits through taxes paid in some other year is shown in the fifth column of the table. The sixth column indicates the net transfers received over the course of life by those who end up receiving more benefits than the taxes they pay, and the seventh column shows the differences between total taxes paid and total benefits received by those who end up being net contributors over the life cycle.

---

[93] Established by the Danish parliament in 1962, the Economic Council is an independent think tank advising the Danish government and parliament on issues of economic policy. A detailed explanation of the method used to estimate lifetime incomes can be downloaded from:
www.econ.ku.dk/pbs/default.htm#Recent%20working%20papers

Table 1: Inter-personal versus intra-personal redistribution in Denmark (1,000 euros, 2002 income levels).[1]

	D1	D2	D3	D4	D5	D6	D7	D8	D9	D10	Average
1. Accumulated lifetime market income	470	795	991	1146	1287	1421	1576	1755	2030	2859	1433
2. Taxes 'reserved' for social insurance	211	277	311	338	363	388	418	454	512	711	398
3. Transfers received over the life cycle	546	521	477	434	399	377	348	324	295	262	398
4. Self-financed transfers received in the same year	155	171	171	168	167	167	167	169	173	180	169
5. Self-financed transfers received in another year	54	101	130	149	159	163	157	143	117	81	125
6. Net transfers received over the life cycle by those who are net recipients (3.-4.-5.)	337	249	176	117	73	46	24	11	4	1	104
7. Net taxes paid over the life cycle by those who are net contributors (2.-4.-5.)	2	5	10	20	37	58	94	142	221	450	104

1. All figures are total amounts accumulated over the life cycle, assuming a zero growth-adjusted real discount rate. The notation DX indicates lifetime income decile X.
Source: Bovenberg, Hansen and Sørensen (2008, Table 1).

Not surprisingly, we see from Table 1 that net receipts from the social insurance system are on average higher among the lower income groups and that net contributions to the system are on average higher among high-income earners. This reveals that some amount of redistribution from the lifetime rich to the lifetime poor certainly takes place. However, the table also shows that even in the top decile of the lifetime income distribution (D10) there are some individuals who receive more benefits than the taxes they pay (witness the positive number in row 6 and column 10), and even at the very bottom of the income distribution some people are net taxpayers on a lifetime basis (see the positive figure in row 7 and column 1).

The table allows us to estimate the average amount of intra-personal redistribution over the individual's life cycle relative to the inter-personal distribution of lifetime income from the rich to the poor. To do so, we focus on the last column in the table showing averages across the entire population. Adding the figures in the fourth and fifth rows of that column, we obtain the total amount of tax paid by the average person to finance social transfers to himself. Dividing this number (169+125) by the figure in the second row of the last column – showing the total taxes paid by the average person to finance social transfers (398) – we find that 74 per cent of the taxes levied to finance social insurance represent intra-personal redistribution over the taxpayer's own life cycle. In other words, only the remaining 26 per cent of total taxes and benefits involve inter-personal redistribution from high to low lifetime incomes. Still, the 74 per cent of the tax bill that taxpayers essentially transfer to themselves distort their behaviour because of the missing direct link between taxes paid and benefits received.

The same pattern of redistribution can be observed in other Western countries. In recent years similar studies of intra-personal versus inter-personal redistribution have been undertaken for a number of other Western countries. Some of these studies experimented with alternative methods of estimation and therefore indicated only an interval rather than a single number for the degree of inter-personal redistribution. The findings from these studies are summarised in Table 2 showing the percentage of taxes collected to finance social insurance programmes that represents intra-personal and inter-personal redistribution, respectively. The strong message from all of these studies is that a very large part of the tax bill merely achieves a redistribution of resources from one stage of the taxpayer's life cycle to another rather than a redistribution from the lifetime rich to the lifetime poor.

Table 2: Intra-personal and inter-personal redistribution via the system of social insurance

Country	Percentage of total transfers representing	
	Intra-personal redistribution	Interpersonal redistribution
Australia[1]	38-52	48-62
Denmark[2]	74	26
Ireland[3]	55	45
Italy[3]	55	45
Sweden[4]	76	24
United Kingdom[1]	71-62	29-38

Sources: 1. Falkingham and Harding (1996). 2. Bovenberg, Hansen and Sørenson (2007). 3. O'Donoghue (2001). 4. Hussénius and Selén (1994).

Redistribution and the Impact of Social Transfers: The Danish Example
While existing social insurance systems do not achieve very much inter-
personal redistribution overall, the amount of redistribution differs
considerably across the various social insurance programmes. The differences
will be estimated to illustrate the redistributive impact of the most important
social transfer programmes in Denmark.

**Figure 1. The concentration curve for a hypothetical social transfer
programme**

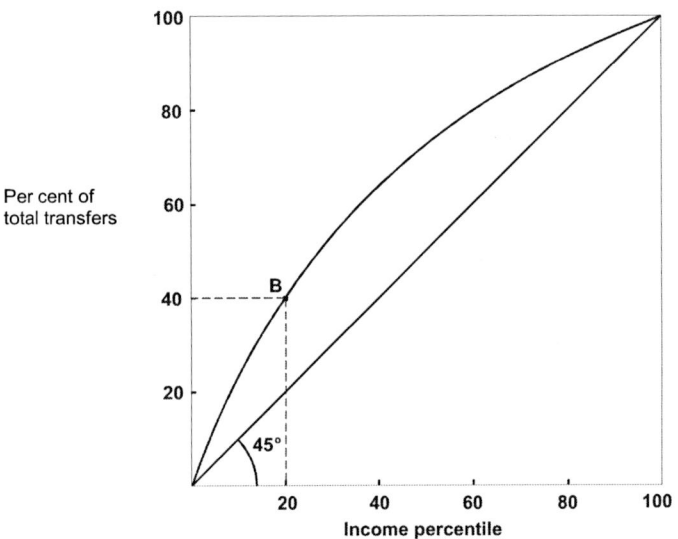

Figure 1 illustrates how one may measure the effect of a transfer programme
on the distribution of income. Along the horizontal axis of the diagram citizens
are ordered in different percentile groups according to the size of their
disposable income. As we move from left to right along the horizontal axis,
disposable income increases. The vertical axis measures the fraction of total
transfers received by the various income groups from some transfer
programme. The so-called *concentration curve* drawn in the diagram thus
indicates the fraction of total benefits received by the poorest X per cent of the
population. For example, point B on the concentration curve shows that the
poorest 20 per cent receive 40 per cent of the benefits paid out under the
hypothetical transfer programme considered. If all individuals were to receive
exactly the same amount of benefit under some transfer programme, the
concentration curve for that programme would coincide with the 45-degree
line, since the poorest X per cent would then always receive exactly X per cent
of total benefits. If the concentration curve for a transfer programme lies above

the diagonal, the benefits from that programme tend to be concentrated among the lower income groups. Such a programme will help to reduce the inequality in the distribution of disposable incomes, compared to a programme that simply pays out the same lump sum benefit to everyone. Hence we may use the area between the concentration curve and the 45-degree line as a measure of the redistributive power of a transfer programme.

The so-called *redistribution indices* shown in Table 3 have been calculated in this way.[94] For each of the transfer programmes considered, the concentration curve and the corresponding redistribution index have been estimated using the distribution of annual disposable incomes as well as the distribution of lifetime disposable incomes. Obviously, the higher the value of the redistribution index, the greater is the redistribution achieved by the relevant transfer programme.[95] In an *annual* perspective, we see that social assistance benefits and education benefits are the most redistributive transfers. Housing benefits and supplementary retirement benefits (which are means-tested) also have a substantial redistributive impact on an annual basis.

Table 3: The redistribution index for Danish transfer programmes, 2002

Transfer Programme	Annual Income	Lifetime Income	Percentage share of total spending on social transfers (2004)[1]
Social assistance	0.70	0.47	6.2
Housing benefits	0.35	0.39	4.4
Disability benefits	0.14	0.39	13.8
Supplementary retirement benefits	0.37	0.19	n.a.
Sickness benefits	0.19	0.18	8.3
Unemployment insurance benefits	0.09	0.11	9.7
Child benefits	0.13	0.10	8.0
Grants to students in higher education	0.68	0.04	5.3
Early retirement benefits	0.00	0.04	10.8
Parental leave benefits	0.22	0.02	0.1
Basic retirement benefit	0.22	0.00	28.1[2]

1. The table excludes a number of minor programmes accounting for 5.3 per cent of total spending on social transfers. Total spending on social transfers amounted to 18.5 per cent of GDP in 2004.
2. Sum of basic and supplementary retirement benefits.
Sources: Danish Economic Council (2005, Table II.5) and Statistics Denmark.

---

[94] To be quite precise, these redistribution indices are calculated as the area between the concentration curve and the diagonal divided by the area below the diagonal (which is ½), so the value of the indices is actually twice the area between the concentration curve and the diagonal.
[95] In the Danish context considered here, all transfers are financed out of general government revenues, so to evaluate the relative degrees of redistribution achieved by the various programmes we do not have to consider how they are financed.

By contrast, in a *lifetime* perspective, most transfer programmes have a smaller effect on income distribution. The exception here is disability benefit which is more redistributive in a lifetime context, because (in Denmark) relatively generous benefits are involved; so in terms of annual income, the disabled are not among the poorest income groups. However, since disability typically involves a permanent loss of earnings capacity, the disabled tend to end up with relatively low lifetime incomes, so in a lifetime perspective disability benefits are more redistributive. A considerable part of housing benefits is granted to recipients of disability benefits. This helps to explain why housing benefits are slightly more redistributive in a lifetime context than in an annual context. Unemployment insurance benefits are also a bit more redistributive in a lifetime perspective, because the incidence of long-term unemployment tends to be concentrated on unskilled groups whose lifetime incomes are relatively low.

In general, the ranking of the various transfers according to their redistributive impact changes significantly as the focus shifts from an annual to a lifetime measure of income. Social assistance remains the most redistributive programme, but its redistributive effect is significantly smaller in a lifecycle context. Transfers such as parental leave benefits and the basic retirement benefit (which is a flat benefit granted to all Danish residents above the age of 65) have a significant impact on the distribution of annual incomes, but exert (almost) the same effect on the distribution of lifetime incomes as an identical lump-sum transfer to all individuals. The reason is that these benefits are granted in a phase of the life cycle when people earn low annual incomes, thereby helping to reduce inequality in annual incomes. However, the individuals who collect these benefits enjoy higher incomes at other times in the course of their life, so these benefits do not contribute much towards narrowing differences in lifetime incomes. The same type of argument holds even more strikingly for grants to students in higher education. While such grants are highly redistributive in an annual context, they have only small effects on the distribution of lifetime incomes.

It should be stressed that Table 3 only measures the degree to which the various transfer programmes systematically redistribute across various income groups. Even if no such redistribution took place, a particular transfer could still result in significant redistribution in other ways in which people differ; for example, child benefits obviously involve a systematic redistribution from childless citizens to families with children. Hence, a low value of the redistribution index in Table 3 does not necessarily mean that the transfer programme in question fails to achieve its intended distributional purpose.

Nevertheless, the fact that many important transfer programmes result in very little redistribution from the lifetime rich to the lifetime poor strongly suggests that the financing and design of these programmes should be reconsidered. Moreover, the fact that many programmes have very different redistributive powers in an annual and in a lifetime perspective indicates the importance of adopting a life cycle perspective on social insurance reform.

The blueprint for social insurance reform presented below is guided by these insights.

How to Reform: Mandatory Savings Accounts

Individual Accounts: A New Model for Social Insurance
In today's system a large proportion of taxes paid by the individual for social insurance is transferred back to him over the life cycle. This may not be perceived because no direct link exists between taxes paid and benefits received. As a result the taxpayer has every incentive to reduce his tax bill (e.g. by working and earning less) and take up social insurance benefits (even if not really needed). However, if a direct link between social security contributions and benefits could be established, these negative incentive effects would disappear, since the contribution would then no longer be a tax, and the benefit would no longer appear as funds transferred from the rest of society. This is the principle of the proposed social insurance reform.

The reform would mean that part of the taxes which currently finance social insurance programmes are replaced by mandatory contributions to individual savings accounts from which certain social insurance benefits would be drawn. In practice the system would operate as follows:

1. An individual account (IA) would be established for each taxpayer.
2. Every year the taxpayer would be obliged to contribute a certain percentage of his gross wage to his IA. The current labour income tax would be reduced by a corresponding amount.
3. Any benefits received under the system would be debited to the holder's IA.
4. Every year the account balance would be carried forward with an appropriate market interest rate (e.g., the after-tax interest rate on government bonds).
5. Any surplus on the IA recorded at the time the taxpayer reaches the official retirement age would be added to his ordinary public pension. Account balances below a certain limit could be paid out as a lump sum; remaining amounts would be converted into an annuity which would be added to the public pension.

6. For individuals with a negative IA balance at the date of retirement, the account balance would be set equal to zero. These individuals would simply receive the public pension to which they are entitled under current rules.

Before addressing the social insurance programmes which should be included in this design, let us take a closer look at the key features of such an individual account system and the advantages it would bring.[96]

Individual Accounts: Insurance
First, the proposed IA system provides *liquidity insurance*: whenever an account holder meets the eligibility criteria for receipt of one of the social insurance benefits included in the system (e.g. unemployment benefit), he can draw the full amount of benefit to which he is entitled even if his account balance turns negative or is already negative. Account holders therefore can never be forced to cut their consumption below the present levels under the current system. Under the account system the government provides the citizen with a credit on a 'rainy day', using his future mandatory contributions to the IA as collateral. For all those citizens who cannot borrow against their future labour income in the private capital market, the government thus provides an essential credit facility allowing them to smooth their consumption over time.

Second, the government offers *lifetime income insurance* via the 'bail-out' clause described in point (6) above. Because negative account balances are cancelled at the time of retirement, citizens are guaranteed the same minimum lifetime income as that offered by the present system of social insurance. The total retirement benefit can never fall below the public pension implied by existing rules, and during his working life a person can collect the same benefits at the same rates and under the same eligibility rules as at present. The negative account balances measure the extent to which these account-holders receive transfers from the rest of society over their working careers, since the negative balances must be covered by general tax revenues. Because the negative account balances reflect the difference between total contributions paid and total benefits collected over the entire active life of the account holder, the 'bail-out' clause implies that redistribution is based on *lifetime* income rather than on annual income, in accordance with the principle advocated earlier. Since contributions to the IA depend on earnings, and since benefits will mainly be drawn from the IA when the account-holder is out of work, the account balance at the date of retirement is a good measure of the account-holder's long-term (historical) earnings capacity. The government effectively offers,

---

[96] Readers with a background in economics may wish to consult Sørensen, 2003 or Bovenberg and Sørensen, 2004 for a more rigorous exposition of the points made in the next two sections.

through the bail-out clause, a minimum lifetime income guarantee protecting the weakest members of society. The government can actually afford to offer such a lifetime income guarantee despite the fact that it must pay out the positive IA balances, because the improvement in work incentives implied by the IA system will strengthen the public finances (see Table 5 below).

The proposed IA system therefore meets the two basic objectives of social insurance discussed earlier: liquidity insurance and lifetime income insurance. In addition, two other characteristics of the IA system should be stressed. First, contributions to the accounts must be *mandatory*, at least as long as the positive account balance does not exceed a certain (high) limit. As already noted, it is the government's power to impose mandatory contributions that allows it to offer liquidity insurance in cases where the private market fails to provide such insurance. In return for offering a credit facility through the IA system, the government must be sure to get its money back from those who can afford to pay back, that is, from those whose long-run earnings capacity enables them to accumulate positive IA balances at retirement.

Second, to prevent abuse of the lifetime income guarantee, account-holders can only draw benefits *under the same eligibility criteria as the present ones*. If IA holders could freely draw from their accounts, they would have an incentive to withdraw as much as possible since the bail-out clause ensures that any negative balance is cancelled at the time of retirement. Obviously the government cannot allow or afford such abuse. It should be noted that these regulations also address problems arising from myopia, lack of self-control, and calculated behaviour. If left to rely on voluntary savings, some people lacking foresight or self-discipline may not save enough even if they could in fact provide insurance for themselves. Moreover, some people may speculate that if they do not save to protect themselves against unexpected income losses, the government will bail them out anyway because it cannot accept to have people starving. The mandatory nature of IA contributions and the restrictions on withdrawals from the accounts limit the scope for this type of behaviour.

Individual Accounts: Providing Incentives
One of the principal aims of such a reform is to reduce the negative incentive effects of the current tax-financed system of social insurance. The proposed IA system would succeed in doing this in two important ways. First of all, for all those who end up with a positive IA balance, the system will *reduce the marginal and average tax rate on labour income*, because part of the labour income tax is replaced by contributions to the individual accounts. Since these contributions are returned to the contributor with interest - either in the form of some future benefit during his working career or in the form of a higher retirement benefit - they are a kind of individual saving rather than a tax.

Hence the IA contributions will not create the same disincentive to work as the current labour income tax. Indeed, for citizens who are forward-looking and not subject to liquidity constraints, the mandatory IA contribution will be equivalent to private saving. These individuals will realise that their IA contributions will be returned with a market interest rate;[97] and by saving less on other accounts or by borrowing, they will be able to adjust their total savings to its desired level, despite being obliged to invest some of their savings in the IA. Thus, for these people the IA contribution will not work like a tax at all.

For those facing liquidity constraints, the mandatory IA contribution will to some extent be seen as a tax, since these persons cannot (by the definition of a 'liquidity constraint') transfer money to the IA from other accounts or borrow to pay the contribution. On the other hand, since these individuals do get their contributions back (with interest) at some later time (when they may also be liquidity-constrained), the contribution will only partly work like a tax, so their effective tax rate on labour income will fall to a degree depending on the severity of the liquidity constraint they face. Finally, for those who do not look ahead at all, living from 'hand to mouth', the mandatory IA contribution may of course be seen like just another tax, generating the same disincentives as the current labour income tax. On average, however, there is no doubt that the IA contributions will create a smaller disincentive to work than the labour income taxes they replace.

The second important incentive effect is that the IA system will *encourage people not to take up social insurance benefits* unless they really need them, since they effectively pay for the benefits themselves in the form of a lower IA balance and hence a lower pension. Indeed, since IA balances are carried forward with interest until retirement, any benefit drawn from the account is fully self-financed in present value terms for people who can look forward to ending up with a positive IA balance. In this sense the replacement rate in the transfer programmes included in the IA system is effectively reduced to zero. Because many of the relevant benefits can be collected only when the recipient is out of work, this self-financing of benefits creates a strong incentive to minimize periods of unemployment and absence from the labour market. As the case study presented below will illustrate, this feature of the IA system will generate an even stronger improvement in work incentives than the cut in the tax rate on labour income. Apart from strengthening the incentive to work, the self-financing of benefits implied by the IA system will also discourage benefit

---

[97] Note that the government only has to pay an *after-tax* interest rate on the IA balances to make saving via the IAs just as attractive as long-term saving in other (non-subsidised) savings vehicles.

cheating and moral hazard more generally, by inducing people to take precautionary action to prevent the occurrence of the social events that trigger benefit payments under the current system.

Of course, these positive incentives will only affect those who expect to end up with a positive IA balance at the date of retirement. Those who expect to end up with a deficit will face exactly the same incentives as under the current tax-transfer system. Due to the lifetime income guarantee built into the system (the 'bail-out' clause), these individuals can collect the same benefits subject to the same constraints as under the current system, and their IA contribution will work just like the labour income tax it replaces since it is not returned to them. Hence these people have no incentive to change their behaviour. It should be noted, however, that some of those who end up with negative IA balances may actually respond to the positive incentives in the system until the time they realise that they will not be able to accumulate a positive balance.[98]

How the System will be Run
What about the administration of the proposed system of individual accounts? Who would run them and under what rules? The system could be run in different ways, though withdrawals from the accounts would be regulated by the eligibility conditions now in force in the current social insurance programmes.

One option is for the government to administer the scheme as a pure book-keeping system of 'notional' accounts. It would keep the records of contributions to, and payments from, each individual account and determine the amount of lump sum or annuity paid out to account-holder at official retirement age. In this scenario the IA system would be run on a 'pay-as-you-go' basis like the current system of social insurance for people of working age - that is, the contributions to the IAs would not be saved and invested in the capital market, even though account balances would be carried forward with the after-tax interest rate on government bonds as a matter of book-keeping.

As an alternative, the government might choose to give individual account-holders the option of leaving the administration of their accounts in the hands of a certified financial institution that invests the account balances in the capital market. In this case positive account balances would be carried forward with the rate of return that the savings can earn in the market. Whenever an account-holder became eligible for one of the social benefits included in the system, the relevant government agency would report to the private

---

[98] On the other hand, there may also be some who do not initially respond to the incentives because they do not expect to be able to build up a positive IA balance, even though they actually manage to do so.

administrator of the account who would pay out the benefit from the account. If the account balance turned negative, the government would transfer a corresponding amount to the account and charge the government bond interest rate on the accumulated amount transferred.

By allowing account-holders this option, the government would give them freedom of choice over the investment of their mandatory savings, constrained by reasonable prudential regulations of the extent to which savings could be invested in risky assets.[99] On the other hand, such a system of 'funded' accounts held in private financial institutions would be likely to involve higher administration and transactions costs than a government-run system of notional accounts which allows the government to reap economies of scale. In any case, taxpayers should always have the option of leaving the administration of their IA to the government as a pure pay-as-you-go book-keeping exercise.

The transition to the IA system could be designed in one of two ways, either phased in for different cohorts, or introduced for all on the same day. Under the first alternative, new young cohorts would become subject to the IA system as they reach a certain age, while the cohorts above that age at the time of reform would continue under the current tax-financed system of social insurance. Under the second alternative, all individuals would become subject to the new IA system from day one. In this scenario people close to retirement age at the time of reform would obviously only be able to accumulate small IA balances, but with the passing of time the IA balances paid out at retirement would gradually increase, as the younger cohorts would have had longer time to accumulate their balances.

Both of these transition strategies would ensure a smooth and gradual phase-in of the new IA system, as the total account balances paid out by the government would build up slowly over time, starting from zero. Even if the IA system were designed as a funded system where account balances are invested in the capital market, it would not involve any significant redistribution across generations. The reason is that payments from the IA system would only include certain benefits for people of working age which would tend to be spread out over a person's working career. Hence people would not have to contribute to the system for years or decades before being eligible for any benefit from the system. This is in contrast to a funded system of old-age pensions which raises a problem of intergenerational fairness if it replaces a pay-as-you-go system of retirement benefits. In that case the young transition

---

[99] Such regulation would be warranted since The Government would have to bail out account holders who lose their assets.

cohorts have to save to fund their own retirement benefits while at the same time paying taxes to support the current transition generation of retirees who did not fund their pensions. The transition to the proposed IA system does not generate a similar intergenerational distribution problem because it does not involve a similar systematic redistribution between young and old.

Designing the Individual Account: The Danish Example
How might the individual accounts be designed in practice? The proposal for an IA system for Denmark put forward by the Danish Economic Council in 2005 provides a good example.[100] It also provides the opportunity to consider which specific transfer programmes should be included in the IA system. The natural candidates for inclusion in the IA system are the transfer programmes for people of working age which involve a high degree of redistribution over the individual life cycle and a low degree of redistribution from the lifetime rich to the lifetime poor. This was the guideline for the proposal from the Danish Economic Council (henceforth the DEC proposal). Specifically, the DEC proposed inclusion of the following transfers in the IA system:

1. Short-term unemployment benefits (for periods of unemployment up to three months)
2. Early retirement benefits
3. Grants to student in higher education
4. Sickness benefits (up to a limited number of sickness days)
5. Parental leave benefits
6. Universal child benefits

The redistribution indices in the second column of Table 3 showed that all the above programmes generate relatively little redistribution of lifetime incomes in the Danish context, compared to programmes such as social assistance, housing benefits and disability benefits. However, from the data underlying Table 3 the DEC found that the degree of lifetime income redistribution implied by benefits paid to workers suffering long periods of unemployment (exceeding three months) is about twice as large as the interpersonal redistribution generated by short-term unemployment benefits (for periods shorter than three months). For this reason the DEC proposal includes only short-term unemployment benefits in the IA system. Similarly, benefits paid during long periods of sickness tend to be more redistributive than those paid during short spells. Moreover, short-term sickness spells tend to be more difficult to verify. The DEC therefore proposed that benefits paid during a limited number of sickness days should be included in the IA system. Child

---

[100] Peter Birch Sørensen participated in the development of this proposal as Chairman of the Danish Economic Council.

benefits included in the system are universal flat benefits paid to all Danish mothers without any means-testing. Single mothers are entitled to additional means-tested child benefits which are more redistributive and are therefore not included in the IA system. For married couples, the DEC proposed that any benefit paid to one of the spouses should be debited by half the amount on the IA of each spouse, and for unmarried parents any child-related benefits would be similarly debited by half the amount on the IA of each parent. These rules are intended to ensure a reasonably equal distribution of IA balances between men and women.

The DEC proposed that the mandatory contributions to the IAs should be a fixed percentage of the base of the Danish payroll tax. This tax is levied on gross wage income and on the imputed labour income of the self-employed (with no cap for any of these groups); for wage earners, the tax is collected at the employee level. Under the DEC proposal, the percentage IA contribution would be set at such a level that total contributions would correspond to total expenditure on the transfers included in the IA system, and the payroll tax would be cut by a corresponding amount, estimated at roughly 8 percentage points. For each individual taxpayer, the mandatory contribution to the IA would thus be offset by a tax cut of exactly the same magnitude.

In addition, the DEC proposal has all the other features summarised in the first part of this chapter, including the requirement that account-holders must meet the current eligibility criteria to receive payments from their accounts, and the 'bail-out' clause that negative IA balances are cancelled at retirement. Through this provision for lifetime income insurance the above six transfer programmes included in the system become targeted at individuals and families with low lifetime incomes, whereas those who end up with positive IA balances effectively insure themselves over the life cycle, while still obtaining short-term liquidity insurance through their ability to draw on their accounts even if the balance is temporarily negative.

The Impact
The effects of the IA system on the distribution of lifetime incomes, the labour market and public finances and economic efficiency can now be summarised.

(i) *Distribution of lifetime income:* The data on lifetime incomes underlying Table 1 allowed the DEC to estimate the impact of the proposed IA system on the distribution of lifetime incomes in Denmark in the hypothetical situation where no one changes his or her behaviour. Although the very purpose of the reform is to induce a change in behaviour, these estimates nevertheless provide an indication of the impact on the distribution of economic welfare.[101]

Table 4 overleaf shows the estimated distributional effects of the proposed IA system in the absence of behavioural changes. The table groups the Danish population into ten income deciles according to the size of their lifetime disposable income obtained under the current tax-transfer system. The numbers shown in the table are based on the current patterns of earnings and take-up of the various benefits across the population. The second row of the table shows that the accumulated contributions to the proposed individual accounts rise relative to the accumulated withdrawals as lifetime income increases. This is not surprising, since contributions are proportional to earned income whereas most benefits are paid out in flat rates independent of income, and since the low-income groups tend to rely more on transfers than the high-income groups do. As a consequence, it can be seen from the third row that the account balances at retirement make up a higher percentage of lifetime income as income increases. Nevertheless, the fourth row of Table 4 shows that even among the poorest 10 per cent of the population (column D1) there are more than seven out of one hundred people who end up with a positive account balance. Moreover, even among the richest 10 per cent of the population (column D10), more than 20 out of 100 individuals end up with a negative account balance. Across the population as a whole, the last column of Table 4 shows that about 46 per cent will manage to accumulate an account surplus if behaviour is unchanged. However, according to the data underlying the table, many individuals would only have to change their behaviour a little bit (working a little more and collecting a little less benefit) in order to accumulate an account surplus. On this basis the DEC estimated that about 60 per cent of the population would end up with a positive IA balance once allowance is made for realistic behavioural responses to the system, discussed below.

---

[101] Indeed, even though Table 4 below neglects behavioural changes, the third column in the table nevertheless indicates the approximate impact of the IA system on the distribution of economic welfare if taxpayers have optimised their behaviour prior to the reform. If people have already adjusted their labour supply to the point where they are indifferent between working a little more and a little less, a small change in labour supply induced by the reform will not have any noticeable impact on their welfare. Hence it is legitimate to abstract from the effects of behavioural changes when we evaluate the effect of the reform on the distribution of welfare.

Table 4: Average payments to and from the individual accounts and account balances at the time of retirement across lifetime income deciles[1]

	D1	D2	D3	D4	D5	D6	D7	D8	D9	D10	Average
Lifetime income (index)	62	79	86	92	97	102	107	113	121	141	100
Accumulated payment into account in per cent of accumulated withdrawal from account	34	56	72	84	97	109	123	141	161	210	100
Account balance at retirement[2] in per cent of accumulated lifetime disposable income[3]	0.1	0.4	0.7	0.9	1.2	1.4	1.8	2.2	2.5	3.3	1.6
Per cent of adult population with positive account balance	7.2	17.1	27.7	36.3	43.0	51.2	57.2	65.8	71.0	79.7	45.6

1. The estimates assume a zero growth-adjusted real interest rate and unchanged behaviour.
2. Average account balance across the entire sample population, where negative account balances have been set to zero.
3. Accumulated income up until the official retirement age of 65; average across the entire sample population.
Source: Danish Economic Council (2005, Table VI.3)

Although Table 4 indicates that the proposed IA system does tend to shift the distribution of lifetime incomes in favour of the better-off, the overall increase in inequality is modest. Inequality is usually measured by the so-called Gini coefficient indicating the fraction of total income that would have to be redistributed from the richest half of the population to the poorest half to achieve complete equality. The Gini coefficient for the distribution of lifetime market incomes in Denmark is currently 0.253, which means that roughly one quarter of total income would have to be transferred from the richest half to the poorest half to ensure that everybody receives the same income before taxes and transfers. When taxes and transfers are accounted for, the Danish Gini coefficient drops to 0.127. Measured by the percentage reduction in the Gini coefficient, the current tax-transfer system thus reduces inequality by an amount equal to (0.253-0.127)/0.253 = 49.8 per cent. According to the DEC estimates underlying Table 4, the proposed IA system would increase the Gini coefficient for the distribution of disposable lifetime income from the current value of 0.127 to 0.133. After the reform the redistribution of market incomes implied by the Danish tax-transfer system would therefore be (0.253-0.133)/0.253 = 47.4 per cent; only a slight reduction compared to the 49.8 per cent of market incomes redistributed through the current system.[102] Moreover, as will be explained below, although inequality would be slightly greater than before, the total amount available for redistribution would increase as a result

---

[102] These mechanical calculations are only approximations since they abstract from the change in the distribution of market incomes that the IA system is likely to generate.

of the reform and no one would be worse off than before, due to the lifetime income insurance provided by the IA system.

(ii) *Labour market and the public finances:* The proposed IA system implies that those who end up with negative account balances pay the same taxes and receive the same benefits as today, while those with positive balances receive an addition to their retirement pension. If behaviour were unchanged, the reform would therefore weaken the public finances as the government distributes the positive IA balances. According to the third row and last column of Table 4, the additional expense for the government would amount to 1.6 per cent of the existing labour income tax base. However, since the reform strengthens work incentives, the labour income tax base will increase, and if this increase is sufficiently large, the government will be able to finance the pay-out of the positive IA balances without having to raise any tax rates.

For those who expect to accumulate a positive IA balance, the reform will strengthen work incentives in three ways: First of all, it will reduce the *marginal* tax rate on labour income (the tax paid on an extra pound of earnings), since the mandatory contribution to the IA will not work like a tax, as explained in above (see p.80). The lower marginal tax rate will encourage those who are already employed to increase the number of hours worked, to the extent that they have the possibility of doing so. We shall refer to this as the *hours-of-work effect*. Second, the IA reform will also reduce the *average* tax rate on labour income - that is, the total tax bill relative to total pre-tax income. This will strengthen the incentive for those who are not currently employed to seek employment, thus increasing the number of people employed. This could be described as a labour force *participation effect*. Third, in the transfer programmes included in the IA system *the effective benefit rate will drop to zero,* since people will finance the benefits themselves in the form of a reduction in their IA balance. Because most of the benefits included in the system are paid out only when the recipient is not working, this cut in the effective benefit rates will also encourage people to reduce the length of the periods during which they are not working. Again, this will create a positive labour force participation effect.

Through these three channels the IA reform will stimulate total employment, thereby boosting the tax base. The reform may also strengthen the tax base in other ways – for example, the lower tax rate on labour income may reduce the fraction of total compensation taking the form of untaxed fringe benefits rather than ordinary taxable income, although such effects are not included in the calculations reported below.

The magnitude of these changes in labour supply, and the impact on the public budget, if the IA system proposed by the DEC were implemented in Denmark, have been estimated in a recent research paper by Bovenberg, Hansen and Sørensen (2007). The effects depend on the sensitivity of hours worked to a change in the marginal after-tax wage rate and on the sensitivity of labour force participation to a change in the net income gain from employment (measured as the difference between a person's net income when employed and his net income when he is not employed). A large body of empirical economic research has tried to estimate the size of these labour supply elasticities. In their evaluation of the employment effects of the proposed IA reform, Bovenberg, Hansen and Sørensen (op. cit.) chose conservative estimates from the low end of the spectrum of estimated labour supply elasticities in the academic literature. On this basis they arrived at the results summarised in Table 5 which shows the estimated impact of the IA reform on the public budget.[103]

Table 5: Estimated effects on net public revenue of including various transfer programmes in the system of individual accounts[1]

Benefit	1. Static effect	2. Hours effect of lower taxes	3. Participation effect of lower taxes	4. Participation effect of lower benefits	5. Total dynamic effect (2.+3.+4.)	6. Total effect on net revenue (1.+5.)
Unemployment[2]	-1.19	0.18	0.57	1.00	1.75	0.56
Early retirement	-0.83	0.24	0.79	2.26	3.29	2.46
Sickness	-0.50	0.07	0.22	0.33	0.62	0.12
Parental leave	-0.06	0.01	0.04	0.10	0.15	0.09
All 4 programs above	-2.58	0.50	1.62	3.69	5.81	3.23
Education[3]	-0.35	0.07	0.24	-	-	-
Child	-0.41	0.11	0.34	-	-	-

Notes:
1. Measured in per cent of the total labour income tax base for individuals with an IA surplus.
2. Only short-term unemployment benefits.
3. Only benefits to study in higher education.
The calculations assume that the average elasticity of hours worked with respect to the marginal after-tax wage rate is 0.05 and that the average elasticity of labour force participation with respect to the net income gain from employment is 0.10.

Source: Bovenberg, Hansen and Sørenson (2007b, Table 3).

---

[103] Apart from depending on labour supply elasticities, the budgetary effects of the IA reform are also determined by the initial tax and benefit rates and the degree to which entitlement to benefits depends on previous employment and previous taxes paid. Bovenberg, Hansen and Sørensen, 2007b explain in detail how all these parameters were estimated for Denmark.

All figures in the table are measured as a percentage of the total labour income tax base for individuals with an IA surplus which amounts to about 60 per cent of the aggregate labour income tax base in the economy. The table shows separate revenue effects for each of the six transfer programmes included in the DEC proposal for an IA system. The first column in Table 5 indicates the 'static' effects on the budget that would occur if there were no changes in behaviour.

These static effects reflect the additional expense the government incurs when it pays out the positive IA balances; they are identical to the DEC estimates of the size of the positive IA balances that would materialise in case of unchanged behaviour.[104] The second column in Table 5 shows the additional direct and indirect tax revenue generated when taxpayers increase their working hours in response to the fall in the marginal tax rate, and the third column shows the additional net revenue produced by the rise in labour force participation that results from the fall in the average tax rate on labour income. For those transfer programmes where benefits are paid out only when the recipient is out of work, there is a further positive participation effect on public revenue, as the IA system induces people to reduce their reliance on such benefits by reducing the time spent outside the labour market. This revenue effect appears in the fourth column of Table 5.

The hours-of-work effect and the participation effects add up to the total 'dynamic' revenue effect shown in the fifth column of the table. This is the overall improvement of the budget generated by the positive labour supply effects of the IA reform. When the static budgetary loss in the first column is subtracted from the dynamic revenue gain, we obtain the total effect on net revenue given in the sixth column. For the programmes in the four upper rows where benefits are conditional on non-employment, it can be seen that the total net revenue gain amounts to about 3.2 per cent of the labour income tax base for those with positive IA balances, or almost 2 per cent of the labour income tax base for all taxpayers.

Education grants and child benefits are not conditional on the recipient being out of work, so the labour force participation effect of reducing the effective benefit rates in these programmes is uncertain. If lower effective education grants induce fewer people to go on to higher education or to complete their studies more quickly, they may enter the labour market at an earlier age. On the other hand, there may be an offsetting negative effect on labour force participation since individuals with less education tend to retire earlier or may

---

[104] The data underlying the first column in Table 5 are thus identical to the data underlying Table 4.

face greater risks of non-employment. A cut in effective child benefits could conceivably reduce fertility a bit, thus causing less absence from the labour market as a result of child bearing and child rearing. However, these indirect participation effects on labour supply are highly uncertain. This is why no estimates for the participation effects of lower benefits are included in the two bottom rows of column 4 in Table 5. Still, including education grants (to students in higher education) and the universal child benefit in the IA system will allow a further cut in the labour income tax rate which will stimulate labour supply. The resulting positive effects on the public budget are estimated in columns 2 and 3 in the two bottom rows of Table 5. It can be seen that the 'dynamic' revenue gains from additional labour supply roughly offset the initial 'static' deterioration of the budget caused by the need to pay out positive IA balances.

Overall these estimates indicate that the positive labour market effects of the proposed IA reform would be more than sufficient to ensure that the reform would be self-financing. Indeed, according to Table 4 there would even be a net revenue gain that the government could use to increase public goods provision, to lower taxes further, or to subsidise the individual accounts of low-income earners to increase their chance of accumulating an IA surplus (see below).

It may sound too good to be true that the IA reform would be self-financing. While it is widely recognised that a tax cut will partly pay for itself by strengthening the tax base, most economists agree that a tax cut will not normally be fully self-financing, given a realistic magnitude of the positive labour supply response. However, the IA system proposed here *combines* a tax cut with a 100 per cent cut in the effective benefit rates in the relevant transfer programmes: since people pay for their own benefits through a cut in their old age pension of the same present value, the replacement rates in the transfer programmes included in the IA system effectively drop to zero. As indicated in the fourth column of Table 5, this generates a strong positive participation effect on labour supply, despite the rather conservative labour supply elasticities assumed.

(iii) *Economic Efficiency:* The IA reform would, at least in the Danish context, make a lot of people better off without making anybody worse off.[105] Under

---

[105] In the jargon of economists, the reform would create a 'Pareto improvement'. Italian economist Vilfredo Pareto (1848-1923) argued that if a policy reform makes some people better off at the expense of others, the scientist has no objective way of judging whether the reform improves social welfare. But if a reform increases the welfare of some citizens without reducing that of any other citizen, then social welfare unambiguously improves, according to the criterion suggested by Pareto.

the proposed IA system, individuals with a negative IA balance will still have access to exactly the same benefits on exactly the same conditions as those prevailing today, so none of them can be worse off under the IA system. Moreover, all those ending up with a positive IA balance – roughly 60 per cent of Danish taxpayers once behavioural changes are accounted for – will experience an income gain in the form of a higher total retirement benefit.

Society's economic gain from the reform results from improved work incentives. The size of this overall gain in economic efficiency can be estimated as follows. The value of the extra output generated by one more hour of work may be approximated by the *pre-tax* wage rate paid to the worker. If the worker has adjusted his labour supply to the point where he is indifferent as between working a little more or a little less, his *after-tax* wage rate will measure the extra income needed to compensate him for the loss of an hour of leisure. The wedge between the pre-tax and the after-tax wage rate therefore measures the social gain from an extra hour of work, since this tax wedge equals the difference between the value of the extra output produced and the value of the leisure given up. Hence the total economic gain from the IA reform may be calculated as the tax wedge times the total increase in employment generated by the reform. But this is exactly the total 'dynamic' revenue gain stated in the fifth column of Table 5. Thus we may use the dynamic revenue gain as an indicator of the economic efficiency gain created by the reform. According to the fifth row and fifth column of Table 5, the total gain from an IA system encompassing short-term unemployment benefits, early retirement benefits, sickness benefits and parental leave benefits would be roughly 5.8 per cent of the labour income tax base for those with positive IA balances, corresponding to about 3.5 per cent of the total labour income tax base. This is a sizeable gain in economic efficiency.

Looking at the gain another way, the public revenue increase will, indirectly, also benefit society. If people had optimised their labour supply prior to the reform, and are indifferent to whether they work a little more or a little less before the IAs are introduced, the rise in employment induced by the reform will not have any noticeable *direct* impact on their welfare. However, the increase in employment does generate additional public revenue which the government may use to offer improved public services or to cut tax rates further. Through this public revenue gain (the 'fiscal external effect' in the jargon of economists) citizens will thus indirectly gain from the reform.

It should be stressed that the dynamic revenue effect only captures the *fiscal* gain from the IA reform; there may be other non-fiscal effects which are important for social welfare from a broader perspective. For example, a parental leave scheme allowing parents to spend more time with their children may have beneficial effects for society if more intensive parental care helps to improve the social and cognitive skills of the children. In that case the number in the fourth row and fifth column of Table 5 will overestimate the positive overall welfare effect of including the parental leave scheme in the IA system. Similarly, there may be positive non-fiscal benefits to the rest of society when a person decides to take higher education or when a couple decides to have a child. If the inclusion of education grants and child benefits in the IA system reduces education activity and fertility, the resulting negative 'external effect' on society must then be offset against the fiscal gains recorded in Table 5.

When choosing which transfer programmes to include in the IA system, the government must therefore carefully consider the objectives of each programme. The IA proposal set out here assumes that, whereas an individual's basic education may have significant positive effects on the rest of society – e.g. by facilitating communication with other people - the positive 'external' effects of higher education are generally not very important - that is, the benefit of higher education is mainly reaped by the student himself in the form of a higher lifetime income and the enjoyment of learning. Moreover, most recipients of higher education grants tend to come from well-to-do middle class and upper class families and tend to end up with a relatively high lifetime income. While (some of) these students may still be in need of the liquidity insurance provided by the IA system, it is not obvious that this insurance should be provided through a direct subsidy. Moreover, in the specific Danish context considered here, higher education is already heavily subsidised, since students generally do not pay any tuition fees. By including higher education grants in the IA system, these grants effectively become targeted at those individuals who end up with negative IA balances because of bad luck during their careers, whereas the rest of the recipients self-finance their grants over the course of their lives.

Similarly, the proposal to include universal child benefits and parental leave benefits in the IA system assumes that fertility is not very sensitive to these benefits or that the effect of an extra child on society is small. It also assumes that the main purpose of these benefits is to provide liquidity insurance to families whose incomes are temporarily low or whose expenditure needs are temporarily high, and to redistribute resources towards families with a low earnings potential to reduce the risk that children raised in these families become disadvantaged by their background.

However, if policy-makers give high priority to boosting higher education, and if they want to redistribute towards families with children in general, and not just towards poor families with children, they may not want to include higher education benefits, parental leave benefits and universal child benefits in the IA system.

There could also be other important non-fiscal benefits for society as a whole from reducing unemployment, which would give the IA scheme wider appeal. For example, economic research strongly suggests that the cut in the effective rate of unemployment benefits implied by the IA system will reduce union wage pressure, thereby reducing involuntary unemployment. This in turn may help to reduce social exclusion and crime. More generally, if non-employment is associated with a loss of self-respect and social skills for some people, the increased rate of employment obtained through the IA system would have positive welfare effects that are not included in Table 5.

Individual Accounts for Social Insurance: The Gains

So far this study has focused on the economic case for social insurance based on mandatory individual savings accounts. It will now consider in a broader way the proposed system of individual accounts from an economic viewpoint and from a social and political perspective.

First, it will compare the IA system to other forms of social insurance and self-insurance against income risks. Second, it will consider whether the expectations are realistic: can the beneficial incentive effects of the IA system really be expected to materialise? Finally, it will address the long-term political implications of social insurance based on individual accounts; how can the economic benefits expected from the IA system be distributed as evenly as possible?

Individual Accounts v. Other Insurance Mechanisms
How do individual accounts compare with other forms of social insurance? In Table 6 a system of mandatory individual accounts with a lifetime income guarantee (a 'bail-out' clause) is compared to three other ways of providing insurance against unexpected income losses: voluntary precautionary saving, a 'Bismarckian' system of social insurance, and a 'Beveridgean' social insurance system. In this terminology a Bismarckian insurance system provides a clear actuarial link at the individual level between insurance premiums paid and the value of the insurance provided, whereas the Beveridgean social insurance system is assumed to be redistributive, involving flat social benefits financed by general tax revenues.[106]

---

[106] While it is common to label such a system as 'Beveridgean', Sir William Beveridge himself actually stressed that social insurance benefits ought to be financed by separate (flat) social security contributions rather than through general tax revenue (see Beveridge (1942)). However, as an important difference compared to 'pure' Bismarckian social insurance, the

Under a system based on voluntary private saving, people are left to self-insure against social events. Obviously this limits the problem of 'moral hazard' discussed earlier, and it also implies a strict actuarial link between benefits and contributions, since people finance their 'benefits' out of their own saving. For these reasons a system based on voluntary saving avoids the disincentives to work and preventive action that are associated with a redistributive public social insurance system. However, a significant problem with voluntary saving is that it does not provide liquidity insurance for those who have not managed to save enough on their own account and cannot borrow against their expected future income. Nor does reliance on voluntary saving address the problem that some individuals may lack the necessary foresight to save enough, or the problem that some people may strategically undersave in the expectation that the government will bail them out. Finally, a system based on voluntary private saving obviously does not provide any redistribution of lifetime income from rich to poor.

Table 6: Comparison of individual accounts with alternatives

	Voluntary saving	Bismarckian insurance	Beveridgean redistribution	Individual accounts
Liquidity insurance	-	+	+	+
Lifetime redistribution	-	-	+	+
Paternalism protecting myopic individuals	-	+	+	+
Actuarial link between benefits and contributions	+	+	-	+/-[1]
Self-insurance limiting moral hazard	+	-	-	+/-[1]

1) + for those who end up with positive account balance; - for those who do not

Compared to voluntary saving, mandatory individual accounts redistribute, offer liquidity insurance and protect individuals lacking foresight or self control (the latter feature is referred to as 'paternalism' in the third row of Table 6). Just like voluntary saving, individual accounts combat moral hazard and limit the disincentives to work for those who can look forward to a surplus on their IAs.

The accounts share with Bismarckian insurance the benefits of liquidity insurance and protection of myopic individuals. They differ from Bismarckian insurance in two important respects. First, the accounts redistribute between the lifetime poor and the lifetime rich by bailing out persons who end up with

---

system envisioned by Beveridge was redistributive since it did not involve an actuarial link between contributions and benefits. For a more detailed discussion of the distinguishing features of Beveridgean social insurance, see Lawlor, 1998.

a negative balance at retirement. The price of this redistribution is that the accounts do not provide an actuarial link for the lifetime poor and therefore do not improve incentives for this group. The second difference from Bismarckian insurance is that the accounts combat moral hazard because insurance benefits are taken out of the individual accounts. The other side of this coin is that, compared to Bismarckian insurance where people receive the full insurance benefit without having to face a cut in their pension, the accounts provide less insurance for people who end up with a positive account balance.

Thus all the different insurance mechanisms have their pros and cons, and an optimal overall system of social insurance is likely to involve some mix of the different mechanisms. The optimal mix will depend on country-specific circumstances (a theme considered in the next section) and on the specific type of risk against which protection is needed. The analysis above indicates that mandatory individual savings accounts are a good way of providing insurance in cases where the moral hazard problem associated with Beveridgean or Bismarckian insurance is likely to be important, and where the income risks insured tend to be evenly spread across the population rather than being concentrated among the lifetime poor. However, no claim is made that the IA system represents the ideal system of insurance against all types of social risks.

Would the Incentives Actually Work?
The positive incentive effects of the IA system arise from the stimulus to people to look forward and realise that their contributions to the IA will be returned to them with interest and that any benefit they withdraw will lead to a corresponding reduction of their pension. The evidence is that in practice many people are not very forward-looking in their behaviour. For example, in a study of consumption behaviour in five OECD countries including the UK, Campbell and Mankiw (1991) found that between 20 and 40 per cent of all income is earned by consumers who tend to live 'from hand to mouth', essentially consuming all of their current disposable income immediately without providing for the future through voluntary saving, whereas the remaining 60-80 per cent of income accrues to consumers who do in fact seem to look forward and try to smooth their consumption over time by saving and borrowing at appropriate stages of their life cycle.[107]

The fact that a substantial minority of consumers appears not to be forward-looking was the main reason why the estimated effects of the IA reform presented in Table 5 were based on conservative assumptions about the reaction of labour supply to the IAs. Indeed, the labour supply elasticities

---

[107] In the United Kingdom, the study by Campbell and Mankiw, 1991 found that about two thirds of all incomes are earned by consumers who behave in a forward-looking manner.

assumed in Table 5 are only about half as large as the ˏtypical elasticity estimates obtained in the academic literature on taxation and labour supply. In other words, even if myopia prevented half of all taxpayers from responding to the incentives embodied in the IA system, the system would still have the positive effects reported in Table 5 if the remaining half of taxpayers respond in a 'normal' way to the changes in tax and benefit rates implied by the IA reform. Moreover, under the IA system each taxpayer would receive a statement of his or her current individual account balance every year. This reminder might help to raise taxpayer awareness about the incentives embodied in the system, thereby increasing the positive behavioural responses.

Since people can draw on their individual accounts even when the balance is negative, the IA system combines liquidity insurance in each individual year with self-insurance over the life cycle. Such a system is attractive when the income risks to which people are exposed are not strongly correlated over time - that is, when a single 'bad year' does not tend to be followed by a lot of future bad years. To illustrate, two unemployment spells of half a year spread out over a full-time working career of 35 years will reduce a person's lifetime income by less than 3 per cent. Seen in a lifetime perspective, this is a small risk against which the individual can easily insure himself via the IA system, since the liquidity insurance provided by the system allows him to maintain a decent living standard during the periods of unemployment. However, if unemployment has serious 'scarring' effects so that one period of unemployment significantly increases the risk of future unemployment, an IA system involving life-time self-insurance against unemployment can be quite burdensome for those who are unlucky to become unemployed due to a recession or some other event beyond their control. Economic research suggests that relatively short spells of unemployment usually do not increase a person's future risk of unemployment significantly, whereas a long unemployment spell may seriously harm a person's future chances of finding a job. This is why the IA system proposed earlier only included short-term unemployment benefits.

The above observations suggest that an IA system will work better in countries with relatively flexible labour markets where unemployment spells are fairly short but spread out over a large number of people, whereas the IA system will be less attractive in countries with regulated labour markets and a sharp distinction between 'insiders' with a high degree of job protection and unprotected 'outsiders' who bear the bulk of the burden of unemployment through long unemployment spells. More broadly, if some individuals are always unlucky and therefore remain poor while others continuously 'strike it rich', the IA system becomes less attractive.

Differences in labour market structures are one reason why social insurance via individual accounts may not work equally well in all countries. Other differences in initial conditions may also affect the magnitude of the economic gains from individual accounts in different countries. For example, the higher the initial tax and benefit rates, and the weaker the link between social security taxes paid and benefits received, the greater are the initial distortions to work incentives, and the greater the economic efficiency gain emerging as effective tax and benefit rates are cut via the IA system. Furthermore, in a country that offers many universal benefits to all taxpayers regardless of their means, the redistribution achieved through the tax-transfer system is likely to involve a high degree of intra-personal redistribution over the life cycle of individuals. As we have seen, in such a setting there is considerable scope for economic efficiency gains through the introduction of IAs. By contrast, in a country relying mostly on means-tested benefits to specific targeted groups, the interpersonal redistribution of lifetime incomes is likely to be greater, leaving less scope for gains through an IA system.

But while the attractiveness of an individual account system may depend on the circumstances of the country, and while the optimal design of the details of the system would undoubtedly differ across countries, several trends tend to strengthen the case for the IA system as time goes by. One of these trends is the changing nature of social risks discussed at the start. Second, the liberalisation and growing sophistication of capital markets in recent decades have improved the ability of many people to smooth their consumption over time through saving and borrowing. By allowing individuals to decouple annual consumption from annual disposable income, well-functioning capital markets make lifetime-, rather than annual, incomes better indicators of individual welfare. This increases the relevance of the IA system where redistribution focuses on lifetime incomes.

A third reason for the increased attractiveness of individual accounts is that they are fully portable between jobs. Hence, this type of social insurance does not tie workers to their initial employer. This facilitates labour mobility and the flexibility of the labour market. It is also consistent with the emancipation of the worker, who becomes more independent of specific employers.

Finally, many social insurance programmes suffer from the problem that it is hard to separate the truly needy from other individuals who do not really need help from the government. Lindbeck (2006) has argued that social constraints on the take-up of benefits are weakened in an environment where many people rely on benefits, so that the take-up rate depends positively on how many people already receive benefits. If this is the case, individual accounts may improve the sustainability of the welfare state by inducing people not to take up social benefits unless they really need them. This helps to support a culture emphasizing personal responsibility.

Distributional Aspects: How Can the Gains from the Reform Be Evenly Shared?
The analysis above showed that even on conservative assumptions about the sensitivity of labour supply to economic incentives, an individual account system has the potential to make a lot of people better off without making anybody worse off. But it also showed that the gains from the reform would tend to concentrated in the middle-income and higher-income groups. Although we saw that the resulting increase in inequality would be small, any increase in the inequality of income distribution might be seen as politically undesirable in itself, even though nobody loses in an absolute sense.

It could be argued that the worsening of the equity-efficiency trade-off described at the beginning forces governments to accept more inequality even if their political preference for equality is unchanged. The pressures on the welfare state arising from globalisation, technological change, demographics, and the changing nature of social risks all increase the economic cost of redistribution, as explained in the introduction. Faced with such pressures, a rational government will choose to pursue less ambitious redistribution policies, because the 'price' of redistributing income has gone up. In other words, when the size of the 'pie' shrinks by more as the government tries to redistribute it, less redistribution is warranted. A conventional reaction to such a situation is to simply cut tax and benefit rates within the existing fiscal framework, but this tends to hurt the poor, not only in a relative but also in an absolute sense. Under an IA system, the lifetime income insurance built into the system protects those with low lifetime incomes from further cuts in their living standards while significantly cutting tax and benefit rates for those who can afford to insure themselves over the life cycle. To put it another way, if economic and social trends tend to worsen the equity-efficiency trade-off, governments should look for policy innovations that may improve the terms of this trade-off. The IA system is such an innovation, allowing an improvement of economic incentives in a manner that does not hurt the lifetime poor.

Despite these advantages of the IA system, there may be understandable reasons why a government might object to the (slight) increase in inequality implied by the IA reform proposal outlined above. In many OECD countries the degree of income inequality has increased significantly in recent decades, in part due to the forces of globalisation and technological change biased against low-skilled workers. In such circumstances any further increase in inequality may be unwelcome. Moreover, there is evidence that people care not only about their absolute standard of living, but also about their living standard compared to the standard enjoyed by others, so those who end up with negative IA balances may feel left behind as they observe many of their fellow citizens accumulate positive balances.

Thus, although inevitable if the IA system is to provide lifetime income insurance, it may be seen as problematic that the system splits the population into those who end up with positive account balances and those who do not. Through this separation individual accounts increase the transparency of lifetime redistribution. This might weaken the political support for such redistribution. A related factor that may work in the same direction is that the middle class no longer benefits from redistribution, which is now more closely targeted at the lifetime poor.

At the same time, however, individual accounts give people a stronger sense of ownership and personal responsibility. This may strengthen popular support for the welfare state and the liquidity and lifetime income insurance it provides. Stronger personal ownership may also make it more difficult for the government to change benefit rules, thereby reducing political risks, including the risk that the government may be tempted to default on its promise to pay out the IA balances, once they have been accumulated after the end of a long working career.

In any case, extending the reach of the IA system to the great majority of the population and minimising the rise in inequality generated by the system are worthy goals of public policy. A step in this direction could be taken by moving the 'default line' in the IA system below zero. This would imply that, instead of only paying out an addition to the public pension when the final account balance is positive, the additional pension would be equal to the amount by which the IA balance exceeds a certain negative threshold. For example, if this threshold were minus £20,000 and the account balance at retirement were minus £15,000, the account-holder would receive an addition to his public pension worth £5,000 pounds. Thus only people with negative IA balances falling below minus £20,000 would be affected by the bail-out clause, so lowering the 'default line' below zero would increase the number of people who would benefit from the IA system.

Of course the government would have to find ways of financing the additional pensions that would be paid out from the IAs. One obvious source of finance would be the dynamic revenue gain from the IA reform which may be substantial. If the government wants to go further, it can choose to finance (a part of) the lowering of the 'default line' in the IA system by imposing a modest tax (say, 5 per cent) on positive account balances. In this way the government could redistribute the gains from the IA system away from people with high lifetime incomes (and hence large positive IA balances) towards individuals with low lifetime incomes (reflected in negative IA balances). While the tax on positive IA balances would weaken the positive incentive effects of the IA reform for those subject to this tax, it would help to finance the lowering of the 'default line', thus improving the incentives for low-income earners by increasing their chance of raising their pension through additional work and reduced benefit dependency.

Through such a redistribution of the gains from the IA reform, the government could ensure that only a relatively small minority of the population would have to rely on the lifetime income guarantee built into the system (the bail-out clause). The lifetime income guarantee implies that, while marginal tax and benefit rates are cut for others, they will remain high for the lifetime poor. This is the inescapable price of redistribution. The IA system can alleviate the trade-off between equity and economic efficiency, but it cannot eliminate it. To offset the relatively weak work incentives of those with the lowest lifetime incomes, the government should focus its active labour-market policies on the bottom of the labour market and use instruments other than financial incentives to activate the lifetime poor. Improving the skills of this group through education and training would be an important part of such a strategy.

In summary, financing some of the current welfare state programmes through mandatory contributions to individual accounts could be a valuable component of an overall social policy package designed to protect the disadvantaged without doing unnecessary harm to the work incentives and the norms of personal responsibility needed to sustain a well-functioning market economy and a cohesive society.

Conclusion
Western countries face a future of demographic and social change. Demands for social protection are rising and with them costs. As populations age, more resources must be spent on income support and health care for the elderly. But the cost of providing social insurance for the working population is also set to rise: globalisation changes work patterns and exposes many workers to new risks.

The upshot is that social insurance schemes, which are aimed at tiding people over periods with income losses, are facing hard times. Their central aim of providing social protection remains irrespective of how they are financed (through taxes, contributions or both). They provide liquidity insurance (cash benefits) when income dries up, and they transfer resources from lucky to unlucky individuals over the life cycle. Even now, however, they suffer from downsides: they can push dependency up by reducing the incentive to find a job (or work to capacity), and the taxes levied to finance benefits tend to discourage work efforts. The problem is that, even though a large proportion of the taxes currently levied to finance social insurance benefits is essentially money that the taxpayer transfers to himself over the life cycle, the taxpayer does not perceive a link between taxes paid and benefits received.

This study proposes an answer to the dilemma. A new Individual Social Account (ISA) would replace part of the present system of benefits to people of working age. It would work like a personal savings account owned by each employee. Each year, taxpayers would contribute a percentage of (untaxed) income; their income tax would be cut by a similar amount. Entitlement would remain as it is now. Though benefits received would be debited from the account, a surplus would be carried forward each year. At retirement, any surplus would be added to the official pension. Those with a negative balance would continue to collect the standard official pension.

The system could be run as a government-administered scheme of 'notional' accounts. Alternatively, individual account holders could be given the option of putting their accounts in the hands of registered financial institutions. The scheme could either be phased in (for different cohorts), or be introduced on the same day for all.

What would the gains be? A calculation of the impact on hours worked and participation rates suggests a fiscal gain due to increased labour supply. The non-fiscal gains would be equally impressive. Unemployment would fall because individual workers as well as their trade union representatives would be motivated to minimise spells of unemployment. The fall in unemployment would give the scheme wider appeal. The scheme would work best where labour markets are flexible and unemployment spells are short but spread over a large number of people.

Overall, the Individual Social Account would continue to protect the disadvantaged. But it would do so with much less damage to work incentives or the personal responsibility needed to sustain both the market economy and a cohesive society.

Bibliography

Beveridge, W., *Social Insurance and Allied Services*, Report by Sir William Beveridge presented to Parliament, November 1942, reprinted London, 1995.

Bovenberg, A.L., and P. B. Sørensen, 'Improving the Equity-Efficiency Trade-Off: Mandatory Savings Accounts for Social Insurance' in *International Tax and Public Finance*, 11, 2004 pp. 507-529.

Bovenberg, A.L., M.I. Hansen and P.B. Sørensen, 'Individual Savings Accounts for Social Insurance: Rationale and Alternative Designs', *International Tax and Public Finance*, 15,1, 2008.

Bovenberg, A.L., M.I. Hansen and P.B. Sørensen, *Individual Accounts and the Life Cycle Approach to Social Insurance*, (Mimeo downloadable at http://www.econ.ku.dk/pbs/default.htm#Recent%20working%20papers), 2007.

Campbell, J.Y. and N.G. Mankiw, 'The Response of Consumption to Income: A Cross-Country Investigation' in *European Economic Review*, 35, 1991 pp. 723-756.

Danish Economic Council, *Dansk Økonomi, Forår 2005* (The Danish Economy, Spring 2005), Copenhagen, 2005.

Falkingham, J. and A. Harding, *Poverty Alleviation versus Social Insurance Systems: A Comparison of Lifetime Redistribution* in *Contributions to Economic Analysis*, vol. 232, Amsterdam, 1996.

Hussénius, J. and J. Selé, *Skatter och Socialförsäkringar over Livscykeln – En Simuleringsmodell* (Taxes and Transfers over the Life Cycle – A Simulation Model). Ds 1994: 86 (ESO), Swedish Ministry of Finance, Stockholm, 1994.

Lawlor, S., *Beveridge or Brown? Contribution and Redistribution: The Real Social Security Debate*, Politeia, London, 1998.

O'Donoghue, C., *Redistribution in the Irish Tax-Benefit System*, Ph.D. thesis, London School of Economics, London, 2001.

Sørensen, P. B., 'Social Insurance Based on Private Savings Accounts' in S. Cnossen and H.W. Sinn (eds.), *Public Finances and Public Policy in the New Millennium*, Cambridge Mass., 2003.

V
Tax Reforms and Social Accounts Incentives for Efficient Re-distribution

Alessio J.G. Brown and Dennis J. Snower

Welfare reform: The problem

One reason why poor people in developing economies remain poor is that they often do not have formal title to the assets that would enable them to own their livelihood, especially land. So they cannot use these assets as collateral to buy the fertilizer and agricultural machinery that would make this land much more productive. According to Hernando De Soto[108] the total value of fixed property held, but not legally owned, by the poor in developing countries as well as in ex-communist countries exceeds $3.9 trillion. That is a staggering amount – twenty times the amount of foreign investment in developing countries between 1989 and 1999. It is nearly a hundred times the amount of development assistance given to these countries over the past two decades. If they had title to the assets which they use, many of the currently poor people would no longer be poor. There would be a massive upturn of economic activity in countries that need it most.

One reason why property rights are so important is that they make assets tangible so that they can be used to buy other assets. Assets that bestow formal title are easily divided among multiple owners, so that the ownership of a house or a factory can be shared among many people, any of whom could sell their share without needing to take the physical asset apart.

At first glance, this may sound like a strange way of introducing the subject of tax and benefit systems and welfare state reform in advanced, industrialised countries like Great Britain, but it is not. The reason is that the citizens of these countries also have a large stock of assets that are not tangible and thus cannot be mobilised in the public interest. We don't have property title to a significant percentage of our GNP because of the way our tax and benefit systems are structured. In Great Britain, for example, 11 per cent of our GNP is devoted to benefits. These benefits include pensions, benefits for low-income groups,

---

[108] Hernando De Soto (born 1941 in Arequipa) is a Peruvian economist known for his work on the informal economy. He is the president of Peru's Institute for Liberty and Democracy (ILD), located in Lima.

disability benefits, child support, unemployed benefits, and so on. We don't have title to many of these benefits, since they are granted on the condition that we become ill, impoverished, incapacitated, unemployed or disadvantaged in other diverse ways. We as individuals see no connection between our tax payments and benefit receipts. We are under no illusion that an increase in our individual tax payments would necessarily lead to an increase in our benefit receipts. In short, we do not retain title to the tax payments we make.

And that leaves us with the same sort of losses as those that people in developing countries face because they don't have title to their land. Consequently, we often handle our welfare services – covering public unemployment and disability insurance, state health care and education, state pensions, and so on – as ineffectively and inefficiently as poor Africans often handle their land.

In most destitute African countries, the potential demand for agricultural produce is rising, as populations grow and there are more mouths to be fed. But the supply of agricultural produce does not rise to meet the demand. In free markets of capitalist economies, supply and demand are generally kept in balance through the movement of prices: if the demand for a product rises, then the price of that product rises as well, and that induces producers to supply more of it. But the poor African farmers, as noted, are commonly unable to do so because they have no ownership in their land. So prices cannot perform their self-regulating, homeostatic function.

The Dysfunctional Welfare State.

There has been a rise in the demand for welfare services over the past three decades, which has not been met by a rise in supply. Due to globalisation, skill-biased technological change and deindustrialisation, the distribution of earnings has become more unequal in many OECD countries; in other OECD countries the employment prospects of skilled workers have risen relative to those of unskilled workers. As a result, there is a greater need for income redistribution. The decline of the extended family over this period has accentuated this need, since the informal social insurance among members of an extended family is often no longer available. As people spend more time in post-school education and retire earlier, there is a greater need for lifecycle transfers. In the large continental European countries over the last three decades, unemployment rates of youth and older workers have risen relative to those of prime-age males. This has augmented people's need to transfer incomes from their mid-years (when they are employed) to their early and late years (when they frequently are not). As populations age, the demands for health services and pensions rise.

But in most advanced, industrialised countries, the supply of welfare services has not responded. On the contrary, on account of budgetary pressures, many governments have sought to roll back the finance and provision of welfare services. So the welfare state is not a self-regulating mechanism. Just as human beings' natural mechanisms are vital for their survival – when I am cold I shiver and that warms me up; when I am hot, I sweat and that cools me down – so such mechanisms are essential for the survival of our welfare state. The way to rescue the welfare state – our health and education systems, our pension systems, our unemployment and incapacity benefit systems – is not to raise taxes on productive people and maintain benefits for unproductive ones. That is counterproductive, since higher taxes reduce incentives to remain productive and encourage international outsourcing, whereas benefits granted on the condition of being unproductive discourage work. As a result, the demand for welfare services would rise even more, while the tax base to finance more welfare services would shrink. What is required, instead, is a policy framework that encourages the supply of welfare services to respond automatically to the swings the welfare demands.

There are several other powerful reasons why the supply of welfare services does not adjust to demand. All suppliers of goods and services, whether in the public or the private sectors, need incentives to adjust their offerings to changing customer needs. The most reliable, unambiguous incentives arrive through the forces of competition. When an organization competes with others, then failure to adapt to the customers will often mean going out of business. It is for this reason that competition is so important to generate an efficient allocation of resources. But most welfare states are government monopolies, insulated from competition. Governments often regulate the markets for health, education and various forms of social insurance to abolish potential competition from the private sector. Thus it comes as no surprise that the welfare services offered are unresponsive to the fluctuating demands.

Another important reason for the failure of supply to match demand for welfare services is that the state suppliers have 'soft' budget constraints. It is common for a variety of welfare services – often including health, education, and social insurance – to be financed wholly or in part by general taxes. Consequently, the suppliers of these welfare services face no strong incentive to bring their costs in line with their customers' needs (assessable, for example, through their willingness to pay). Not only does this make the state provision of welfare services inefficient in its own right, it also serves to eliminate private sector competition, since private sector providers generally have 'hard' budget constraints, requiring them to align costs and benefits.

A further reason is the tendency for governments to confuse the requirements of efficiency with those of equity in the provision of welfare services. The unemployment and incapacity benefit systems, for example, are meant to function as a form of insurance against unemployment: the unemployment and incapacity benefits are to be interpreted as pay-outs of this insurance and the tax receipts used to finance these benefits could be viewed as insurance premiums. At the same time, however, these systems are also meant to redistribute income from rich to poor. Thus the 'insurance premiums' are not positively related to the underlying risks; on the contrary, people who are prone to unemployment and disability tend to make lower, not higher, 'premiums'.

We do not wish to suggest that the long-term unemployed or incapacitated should be made to pay higher taxes than their long-term employed counterparts; that would be outrageously inequitable. But we do wish to suggest that governments should think more carefully about how to redistribute income efficiently. It would be far more efficient to redistribute income through the income tax system than through the unemployment benefit system. The reason is that, subject to various partial exceptions, unemployment benefits are awarded on condition of being unemployed, and thus they encourage people to remain unemployed, but income taxes do not have this characteristic. The same point may be made about a variety of further welfare services. Although the health, education and training systems are also used to redistribute income, these redistribution mechanisms are also far less efficient than the income tax system.

Not long ago, a German journalist asked us whether we thought it scandalous that a rich CEO should pay as much for her health insurance as her secretary. We responded by agreeing, 'Yes, that's a scandal, and it's a scandal that she has to pay as much for her automobile insurance. It's also a scandal that when she goes to a restaurant, she isn't asked to report her income, so that the price of her meal can reflect her impressive purchasing power'. There are many ways of redistributing income: through restaurants, car insurance, health insurance and so on. But none of these is particularly efficient. Governments should make great efforts to redistribute income in ways that do least damage to people's incentives to work, to educate and train themselves, and to save and invest.

A system of welfare accounts

Thus far we have argued that our present-day welfare state is inefficient and unresponsive to people's welfare needs because people have no property rights in their welfare services. If people 'owned' the funds that finance their unemployment and incapacity benefits, their education and training programmes, their health services and their pensions, then they would have strong incentives not to waste these funds. While efficiency in the supply of welfare services would clearly improve, these property rights would need to be defined in a way that permits sufficient income redistribution to meet the government's equity goals.

The proposal for policy is to restructure the welfare state so as to create such property rights. In particular, our proposal is to replace the current structure of welfare services by 'welfare accounts'. We propose giving every adult four accounts:

- an *unemployment and incapacity account* instead of the current unemployment and incapacity system,
- a *human capital account* instead of the current system of state post-school education and training,
- a *health account* to insure us against any sickness or disability, and
- a *retirement account* to replace state pensions.

Although at first glance this may sound like a radical – perhaps utopian – proposal, it is not. In fact, the welfare accounts could be structured to reproduce all the main regulations and provisions of the current welfare system. In this way the existing welfare system would be treated as a welfare accounts system: taxes that finance the various current welfare services would be people's contributions to each of their welfare accounts and the receipt of welfare benefits and services would be withdrawals from the welfare accounts.

There would be mandatory minimum contribution rates to each account for each individual, and mandatory maximum withdrawal rates, in line with the current welfare state provisions.

In line with current redistribution systems, the government could tax the account contributions of the rich and subsidise the account contributions of the poor. Welfare systems that are currently run on a pay-as-you-go (PAYG) basis – such as the unemployment, incapacity, health and education systems, where current taxes are used to finance current benefits – could be converted to welfare accounts that are also structured as PAYG. In that event, the welfare accounts would implement redistribution not only between income classes, but also between generations.

Furthermore, individuals would be allowed to make transfers among their accounts. At the end of their working lifetimes, a person could take the balance left in his or her unemployment account or human capital account and transfer it to his or her pension account or health account. If the balance in one account falls to zero, it could be replenished with excess funds from the other accounts.

People could make voluntary contributions, above the mandatory minimum contribution rates, in order to purchase more than the basic minimum levels of welfare services. Whereas contributions would be taxed or subsidised in accordance with incomes, the withdrawals from these accounts and the capital income funded accounts would be taxed at preferential rates. All the government's redistributions among accounts would be balanced budget redistributions. Thus the welfare accounts would be a closed system, in which the sum of the account subsidies would be equal to the sum of the account taxes.

The government would permit negative balances on the human capital accounts, and individuals with negative balances could be required to repay their debts on an income-dependent schedule, along the lines of current loans for university education in the UK.

Why, you may ask, do we need welfare accounts at all? Wouldn't it be preferable simply to rely on individuals' private savings? There are two solid answers. First is moral hazard: knowing that the government will always support the needy regardless of whether they save or not, individuals will have insufficient incentive to save. The welfare accounts force them to save more. Second is redistribution: as noted, funds are to be redistributed in line with current welfare provisions.

Furthermore, you may ask, why should we replace the current structure by welfare accounts? Although the taxes and transfers associated with the welfare accounts could replicate the current redistribution scheme, the accounts would provide greater incentives for productive activity. How this is possible is most easily seen if we start by focusing on unemployment accounts:

Unemployment Accounts.
Once we reinterpret the unemployment benefit system in this way the unused, remaining balances on an individual's unemployment accounts at the end of the working life are fully expropriated. As the system now stands if a worker

has been employed throughout the entire working life and made contributions but never withdrew anything, he or she will not get anything back. Under unemployment accounts, though, the remaining, positive balances are not fully expropriated. Workers will receive a partial refund which can be used to top up their pensions.

Clearly, this government refund in form of a pension top-up must generate employment incentives: the longer you have worked and the less you are unemployed the higher the balance on your account and thus, your refund. If the resulting incentives are strong enough the account system will be self-financing.

Our recent study, by Michael Orszag and us,[109] estimated that the introduction of unemployment accounts in Germany would raise the incentive to work sufficiently to be self-financing and to halve the unemployment rate, whereas in France the unemployment rate would fall by 36 per cent and in Italy by 34 per cent. We assumed that workers who could not finance their unemployment benefits out of their own accounts would receive support under the existing terms and conditions, such that the unemployed would not be worse off than they are in the existing system.

Lastly, you may ask, how do the incentives differ? One way to look at the incentives is by concentrating on the two objectives of the unemployment benefit system: on the one hand it is meant to provide insurance against the income loss of unemployment and on the other hand to redistribute income. Contributions to the unemployment benefit system can be seen as insurance premia and the unemployment benefits can be seen as insurance payouts. To avoid disincentives from insurance in the light of adverse selection or moral hazard, 'good risks' need to be rewarded and 'bad risks' need to be punished. This can happen, for example, in the form of payout-dependent insurance premia and deductibles: the people with low risks of unemployment pay lower contributions and workers have the option of self-financing an initial period of unemployment in return for lower contributions. Such optimal insurance contracts though can not be implemented together with the second objective of redistributing income. Thereby, redistribution creates disincentives to work.

In contrast, unemployment accounts enable the use of incentive instruments for rewarding good risks, namely the pension top-up or refund of a fraction of the positive account balances on retirement. Thereby, people gain and have property rights on their unemployment benefits. But at the same time they also

---

[109] See Brown et al. 2008.

allow the goal of redistribution to be met more efficiently, as pointed out above, by taxing contributions of the rich and subsidizing contributions of the poor, as it depends on income instead of employment status.

Another way to look at the incentives is to interpret the current unemployment system as rewarding people for being unemployed and penalising them for being employed. When an unemployed person finds a job, much of the benefits are withdrawn, particularly for low-wage, unskilled people, and taxes are imposed. The unemployed impose a cost on the employed, since the latter pay the taxes that finance the unemployment benefits of the former. Thus the current unemployment system reduces the work incentives of both the employed and unemployed. By contrast, unemployment accounts alleviate this externality for when an unemployed person makes withdrawals from his unemployment accounts, he is thereby diminishing the amount of funds that are available to him later on.

The unemployment accounts internalise the externality created by intrapersonal redistributions, i.e. of workers contributing in respect of their own benefits. The traditional unemployment benefit system involves both interpersonal redistribution (the contributions of the employed help finance the benefits of the unemployed) and intrapersonal redistribution (a worker's contributions during periods of employment help finance his own benefits during his periods of unemployment). Under the existing unemployment benefit system both types of redistribution are associated taxes and transfer, thereby, with disincentives. In contrast unemployment accounts internalise the externalities from intrapersonal redistribution (workers finance their unemployment out of their unemployment accounts) and thus create higher employment incentives.[110]

The other welfare accounts generate similar incentives and grant property rights:

Training services are analogous to withdrawals from human capital accounts, and the taxes that finance these services are analogous to contributions to the human capital accounts. Human capital accounts could increase people's employability. These accounts could enable people to retrain whenever they considered it appropriate, in response to the ever-changing demands of globalisation and technological advance. Only those people who recognise that it is worth investing in themselves would spend money out of their human

---

[110] It is on account of the interpersonal redistribution that people are refunded only a *fraction* of their final-period account balances; the rest is redistributed to others.

capital accounts. They would reason that the higher wages they earned through their additional skills would more than compensate them for the loss of funds in their human capital accounts. The rest of the account holders would keep their account balances and use them to top up their pension accounts or health accounts once they were retired. This would in general be an efficient use of resources, since individuals know better than the government when it is worth investing in themselves.

Under the current healthcare system, people use health services wastefully, since they do not internalise the costs of these services. Yet if they had health accounts, they would need to weigh the value of these services against their costs, since they would pay their health insurance premiums out of these accounts. They would have more freedom of choice, since they could choose their health providers freely, creating competition between the public and private sectors.

The introduction of retirement accounts could be accompanied by further reforms: the minimum retirement age would be linked to changes in life expectancy, and people would have the opportunity to choose voluntarily whether to work beyond this retirement age. The presence of retirement accounts would permit policy makers to think more rationally about how the incomes of pensions should be adjusted to unexpected changes in external circumstances, such as oil price shocks or exchange rate shocks. Whereas such shocks are borne unequally by the population under the current system, retirement accounts would permit governments to spread the costs equitably across the population, whether working or retired.

How the system would work

How can the UK move from the present benefit dependency system to a framework for unemployment accounts?[111] What are the political or administrative difficulties that would need to be overcome? Which of the existing rules, regulations and procedures would need to be changed? The answer is very simple: none. Neither the contributions and benefits nor the rules and conditions for eligibility, duration of payment, the amounts paid, taxes and transfers need to change.

Only one simple, new provision need be added: at the end of his or her working life, each individual can gain access to a portion of the balance that remains on the unemployment account. The individual might get this amount

---

[111] We have provided a detailed account of how to introduce unemployment accounts in Germany in a paper together with Alfred Boss, see Boss et al., 2008.

as a lump sum, an annuity that tops up the pension or, if available, transfers to his or her health account.

To implement this provision, it will be necessary to keep track of the individual's contributions (including any taxes that fund unemployment insurance) and withdrawals (unemployment benefits paid) in order to calculate the individual's unemployment account balance at the end of his or her working lifetime.

While this accounting exercise may involve some cost – that of installing the relevant information system – it is worth keeping in mind that this policy will inevitably be very popular among the electorate. The reason is that the vast majority of employed people, who pay contributions while making few, if any, withdrawals, are dispossessed at the end of their working lives: they receive none of the difference between the present value of their contributions and the present value of their withdrawals. Under unemployment accounts, by contrast, they would gain access to a portion of this difference. In short, the proposed unemployment accounts system gives them a pay-out, while the current unemployment benefit system does not.

How is this payout to be financed? The electorate should know what is at stake. The answer is simple: by providing this extra payout, the unemployment accounts system creates new employment incentives. Whereas the current unemployment benefit system rewards unemployment (through the unemployment benefits) and penalises employment (via the contributions necessary to finance the unemployment benefits), the unemployment accounts system rewards work. For the longer a person is unemployed, the greater are the associated withdrawals, and the lower is the account balance available to that person at the end of his or her working lifetime. The new employment incentives created through the unemployment accounts system lead people to generate new goods and services, which in turn generate more income. The taxes on this extra income, combined with reduced unemployment benefits paid, finance the extra payout from the unemployment accounts system.

In short, the unemployment accounts system provides an extra pay-out or 'free lunch'. A well-known principle of mainstream economics is, however, that 'there ain't no such thing as a free lunch' in free market economies. But this principle only holds in the absence of economic inefficiencies generated through government interventions, public goods, and the like. The current unemployment benefit system is a massively inefficient government intervention, since the unemployment benefits reduce the unemployed people's incentives to work and the contributions that finance these benefits reduce the employed people's incentives to work. Replacing this system by a more efficient one – unemployment accounts – reduces the amount of waste in the economy and releases new productive activity. The income from this new activity can be used to provide the extra pay-out (the 'free lunch') from the unemployment accounts system.

This, you might think, sounds OK in theory, but how can we be sure that the extra employment incentives will be sufficiently large to enable us to provide the specified extra payout? To answer this question, the employment incentives must be evaluated. In a recent empirical study,[112] we show that, for very conservative estimates of people's response to unemployment accounts, the resulting employment incentives are more than sufficient to finance a substantial payout for those with positive balances, while guaranteeing that those with zero balances receive no less than they do under the current unemployment benefit system.

Furthermore, there is the well-known, infernal problem of transition to the new system. Like traditional pension systems, the current unemployment benefit system is run on a pay-as-you-go (PAYG) principle, whereby the current contributors finance the current recipients of unemployment benefits. Does a switch from the current system to the accounts system mean that the current generation pays twice – past contributions to the current system and further contributions to finance the payout from the accounts system? The answer, for two reasons, is No.

First, the unemployment accounts system can be run on a PAYG basis, so that the contributions of the currently employed people pay the benefits and terminal pay-out from the accounts. There is no need to make the unemployment accounts fully funded – although policy-makers may wish to pursue this course in the longer run. Second, under these circumstances, the transition generation does not pay twice, provided that its right to the terminal pay-out is adjusted pro rata to take account of the length of time over which contributions are made.

A simple example can clarify the second point: Suppose that Person A, who enters the workforce after the unemployment accounts system has been introduced – and who works continuously for 40 years, contributing £1000 per year, before retiring. Then, under the simplifying assumption that the interest rate is zero, his account balance at the end of his working life is £40,000. In order to pay the benefits of people with zero balances and undertake the

---

[112] See Brown et al. 2008.

existing amount of redistribution, suppose that this account balance needs to be taxed at the rate of t. Then Person A's terminal payout is (1-t) x £40,000.

Next, consider Person B, who also works continuously for 40 years before retiring, but who has spent the first 20 years under the old unemployment benefit system and the last 20 years under the unemployment accounts system. Then Person B's terminal pay-out is (1/2) x (1-t) x £40,000, since she has only spent half his working life under the accounts system.

Finally, as noted, it is possible to convert the unemployment accounts system from PAYG to a fully funded system. Recall our finding that the employment incentives are more than sufficient to fund the terminal pay-out for people with positive account balances while guaranteeing that people with zero balances receive the same benefits as under the current system. These 'surplus' incentives can be used to finance the transition to the fully funded system, without requiring the transition generation to pay twice. The transition period, however, would have to be sufficiently long to permit the surplus employment incentives to cover the transition cost.

The advantages: Efficiency and fairness

Although, as noted, the welfare accounts could replicate the provisions underlying the current welfare system, their most important potential contribution – in our opinion – lies in the policy reforms to which they would lead. By making redistributions among account-holders transparent, the account system would generate political pressure to modify these redistributions in accordance with the public interest. For example, in the current welfare system, the redistributions do not go primarily from the rich to the poor. The lion's share of the redistributions takes the form of lifecycle transfers, mainly from the middle years to the early and later years. For most European countries, 20-25 per cent of social transfers actually redistribute income between individuals (interpersonal redistributions), and the remaining 75-80 per cent transfers income across people's lifecycles (intrapersonal redistributions). The welfare account system would give people incentives to conduct these intra-personal, inter-temporal transfers as efficiently as possible. By contrast to the current welfare system, the account system would give people property rights in these inter-temporal transfers. This would enable the government to refocus welfare provision on the 20-25 per cent of transfers devoted to inter-personal redistribution.

The welfare account system would also promote competition in the provision of welfare services. The private sector has an incentive to contribute to the welfare state only if it is impossible for the government to use the tax and transfer system to drive the private providers out of business. This is what happens in the current welfare system. But under the welfare account system, the government could not do so, since its welfare expenditures would have to be financed exclusively from the money it receives out of people's welfare accounts. Then the private and public sectors would compete on a level playing-field.

The standard argument against accounts is that they endanger social solidarity. We would argue that the current system, with its steadily increasing contribution rates and arbitrary benefit cuts, is a much greater threat to social cohesion and solidarity. Welfare accounts would be much more transparent, and that would enable us to achieve our redistributive aims much more effectively.

Since welfare accounts would be more transparent, they would enable politicians to build coalitions of voters favouring the account system, so long as the government guaranteed to maintain existing benefits for existing recipients. Welfare accounts would be popular among young people, who have little confidence that the current system would support them adequately if they become needy. Under these circumstances, a government's ability to renege arbitrarily on its obligations to society could be curtailed.

Welfare accounts promote adaptability by giving people property rights in welfare services. These property rights enable people to internalise more of the costs and benefits of the welfare services and thereby they induce people to use these services more efficiently and adjust them automatically to their changing employment, skill acquisition and pension needs.

For all these reasons, welfare accounts would enable countries to provide welfare services more efficiently and equitably. The entitlement to tax payments would lead to much needed incentives and make for a more efficient tax system.

Bibliography

Boss, A., A.J.G Brown and D. Snower, 'Beschäftigungskonten in Deutschland', *Perspektiven der Wirtschaftspolitik* 9, 2, 2008 pp. 139-155.

Brown, A.J.G., C. Merkl and D. Snower, 'Globalisation and the Welfare State: A Review of 'Can Germany Be Saved?'', *Journal of Economic Literature*, 47,1, 2009 pp.136-158

Brown, A.J.G., M. Orszag and D. Snower, 'Unemployment Accounts and Employment Incentives', *European Journal of Political Economy* 24, 3, 2008 pp. 587-604.